Car Boot Tales

by Paul J Rose

A huge to thanks to my editor, Andrew Males, author of *26 Miles to the Moon*, available now on paperback and Kindle on Amazon: https://www.amazon.co.uk/26-Miles-Moon-Great-Space-ebook/dp/B073DBGY5Y

For Shelly

Contents

Prologue – Every Hero Needs an Origin Story

They say it takes 10,000 hours to become a true master in any given field. If that's true, then I'm a good 9,500 hours away, so let's dispense with the idea of my thinking of myself as any kind of expert, and instead, give you a little bit of background on how this book came into being.

Many years ago, armed with nothing more than a car full of unwanted junk and a wallpaper pasting table, I took myself to my first ever car boot sale. For our American friends, it's a lot like a yard sale, but the difference in name is nothing to do with the metric system.

Over the course of several hours, I saw my pile of stuff slowly diminish and my collection of coins and notes grow larger. At the end of my first sale, I had made close to £200! It felt good. So good, in fact, that I elected to do it again.

And again.

And again. And it was not long before items in my home that used to be labelled as 'rubbish' became relabelled as 'stock'.

I had developed a taste for market trading at the grass roots level. This wasn't flashy city operators in £2000 suits shouting at each other until the buzzer sounded. Oh no – this was working amongst the real people – the people who think nothing of offering £2 for a perfectly functioning games console, or 50p for a pair of shoes.

It was then that something interesting happened. I felt that some of the exchanges I'd enjoyed were worthy of sharing with the world at large. Such genius negotiations must surely serve to educate the economy and help it thrive?

Well no. I had quickly arrived at the conclusion that these people were, in all fairness, complete morons, and I decided to share their stupidity on Facebook, purely as a means to vent my own frustration and to perhaps raise a few giggles along the way.

And raise a few giggles they did. In fact, enough giggles to the point where people asked me for more, and the only way to get more stories was to attend more car boot sales, which led to friends, family and a few random strangers thinking of me as some sort of expert.

"You should write a book!" they proclaimed, and so here it is. A book for anyone who's looking for guidance on how to make the most of parting with their junk, or simply for those who enjoy a good bit of people watching whilst they enjoy feeling their own intellectual superiority over people who, and let's be honest, really should never be left near heavy machinery on their own.

What you should know is that every one of these stories is real. Granted, my own internal monologue may have been expanded upon for comedic purposes, but everything that is shared with you here actually did happen. I feel the need to tell this to you now because later on, you will find the stupidity of some of these people will cause you to bring their authenticity into question.

Now I cannot thank these people personally – I don't know who any of them are, and if, by some bizarre coincidence, you find yourself reading this and thinking "Hey, I remember that guy!" Then I thank you for being part of my journey, and for the 5p that you just spent to pick this up second hand at a car boot sale.

In the vain hopes of putting this book together in an order that will make sense, you'll find that we will often digress. A lot. But then again, if you are planning on spending several hours in a field parting with your no-longer treasured possessions, then your mind is hereby given permission to wander, as mine so very often does.

And with that, fellow Booter, I wish you the very best of luck.

Chapter 1 – Ingredients

So you're planning your first car boot sale. Congratulations – you've entered an exciting new chapter in your life, one filled with exhaustion, frustration and everyone you care about questioning your mental health – well done! Don't worry – I promise you it's going to be worth it.

Let's start at the very beginning, which is not only a very good place to start but is, by its very definition, probably the only place, unless you're telling one of those stories which is actually all a flashback, in which case you start near the end and then cleverly work your way back up to that point. Then again, do we really think that Hollywood is crying out for some intricately woven script about someone selling off old saucepans in a field? I suspect not.

In order to hold a stall at a car boot sale, you will need the following things:

1. A car – and preferably one with a big enough boot and back seat to hold a lot of stuff. Don't try hiring a van – you're already racking up more expenses before you start. A van attracts a higher entry fee than a car, plus the customers (we will find other names for them later) will think you're a pro and may well give you a wide berth – again, I'll explain more later.
2. Some stuff. Now you may well want to go down the route of having some kind of niche stall and that's all well and good, but the majority of us just have a lot of stuff that we want cleared out of our house. Now I fully appreciate that 'some stuff' is an incredibly vague description, but you are only on the opening pages of this book – if this were a movie, you wouldn't have even finished your nachos yet, so calm down – we're getting to it.
3. A folding table. You can pick up a pasting table at your nearest DIY store or if you really want to impress the punters (still looking for a decent collective noun for them, don't worry, it'll come to me) then invest in a heavy-duty folding table which should set you back around £40. Bear in mind that such an investment is for someone planning on doing at least three boot sales before deciding he or she has had enough.

4. An understanding partner. In order to get the best pitches at a car boot sale, you need to get there early – I'm talking stupid early, farmyard early, 'some of us are just getting in from the night before' early. This means waking up at "Oh Jesus" o'clock, going through the short mental ritual, "Just five more minutes, what difference would that really make anyway?" in your head before rolling out of bed, which will invariably wake up your sleeping partner and reset your Brownie Points score to at least a zero, although more realistically, somewhere around minus 3. We'll talk more about how to make this all less horrible later on.

5. A money apron or bum bag – a fashion faux pas to be sure, but they are very practical when it comes to quickly dispensing change, and dispense it you will, because the chances of your buyers having the right change on them are unbelievably slim. No really – stupid slim. Don't be at all surprised to find your first customer offering you a £20 note for something they've just agreed to buy for 50p, and tough luck if you can't make change!

6. A book. The morning is not going to fly by, and when there's every possibility of being pitched next to a fellow stallholder who becomes your new best friend, the reality is that there will be periods of undeniable boredom. Yes, you can play games on your phone if you want – I'm not judging, but you may get a lot of glare from the sunshine and so won't be able to see anything, plus of course you'll be killing your battery in the process, so a good book makes for a sensible time filler.

7. A folding chair. Long before your brain packs up, your feet will, and whilst you can just sling open your driver's door and sit in your car, it's so much nicer to just sit behind your stall and greet your customers as they approach your assorted treasures.

8. A sense of humour – which is the reason I wrote this book. Throughout the course of your morning you are going to enjoy some of the best people watching you can ever hope to encounter, and what's more, the whole experience is going to be interactive. The whole spectrum of humanity will be laid bare before you – from the sublime to the utterly ridiculous – and if you can keep your cool whilst someone attempts to give you 20p for a coat that originally cost you £100, then you are in for a fantastic ride.

And let's face it, this book is all about point number 8. Sure, you're going to pick up some valuable tips as you read through this thing, but we all know that you really came here to laugh at the animals – didn't you?

Chapter 2 – Some Stuff – an Explanation

So just how much junk is there?

A car boot sale is, amongst many other things, a truly cathartic experience. However, before you can truly purge yourself of that original 12" single of "Agadoo" from your shelves, you first have to do some serious soul-searching, and this is especially true when selling off any old gadgets. It might seem simple on the surface, but that calculator you haven't used in twenty years got you through some tough exams in school – are you really ready to part with it just yet?

Gadgetry falls into two main categories once consigned to the loft/shed/cupboard under stairs/parents' house and they keep asking when you're finally going to take it out of there, given that you did move out fourteen years ago - so you better do something about it. These are:

1. Stuff that may well prove useful in the future and is therefore worth keeping somewhere just far enough out of sight that it won't be forgotten.
2. Stuff that will absolutely, unequivocally, you'll stake your life on this one – never be used by you again ever.

Now the first one is tricky. In truth, we can never really know if something will prove useful in the future, or if indeed, left alone long enough, will fall into the realms of vintage tech and become worth thousands. Although the money will pale into insignificance compared to the amount of "Well I hate to say I told you so" tokens you will earn. Hold onto those tokens – they genuinely increase in value the longer you choose not to cash them in, and if used wisely, can bring abrupt victory in the face a force 9 argument. To be fair, the line "Well I hate to say I told you so" is an outright lie. You don't hate saying it, you flipping love it, as well you should!

And let's talk about that 'out of sight' location that I mentioned. This is where you have to be honest. Are you about to put the item back into the same corner of the loft, blissfully aware that the next time you see this item will be when you're preparing for your next car boot sale?

Be a little more ruthless. If you feel its value could genuinely increase over time, then it would be wise to invest in a nice plastic box in which to keep it. It doesn't have to be anything fancy – just enough to keep the dust, spiders and bats away (your loft really is quite a scary place, isn't it?) If it is electronic, then take it out, plug it in, or insert some batteries, and check to see if it actually works.

Now I don't have a crystal ball. I can't tell you that holding on to that mint condition Hungry Hungry Hippos will one day make you a millionaire. However, a simple check on any of the well-known online auction sites will tell you if something is worth holding on to. Beyond that, it really comes down to just how much space you have in your loft.

Those same well-known online auction sites who have not paid me to advertise so will not be getting a mention, advise that the average household has around £4000 of unwanted stuff in it at any one time. That statistic is bound to get you excited, but be warned – just because you paid £150 for that child's car seat originally, don't think you're getting anywhere close to that back – not, at least, at a car boot sale.

It's important to remember a bit of a cliché at this point – "One man's junk is another man's treasure". You need to adopt a certain mindset when it comes to working at a car boot sale, and it's this:

These people are paying me to clean my house.

Just think about that. The stuff that you have brought with you has a personal value to you of zero – you don't want it anymore and so are therefore looking to get rid of it. If you can make some money in the process, well that's great, but ultimately you must remember why you are there – to clear away stuff that you no longer want.

Now ascribing an actual value to a lot of your stuff is tricky, but you do need to have a price in mind. As you'll discover later, merely asking people to make you an offer simply won't work. Now the good news is that truly keen buyers know that the best deals are available first thing in the morning; they'll arrive early and are ready to deal, but that doesn't mean you need to accept their low offers – if you really feel strongly that a certain item should go for a certain price, then hold out for a while. If they recognise a good deal, they'll be back, and if not, you can always lower the price later in the day.

Actually, that gives me a wonderful opportunity to tell a story which illustrates my point. First, permit me just a little digression.

You see, there's nothing wrong with being a little cheeky. In fact, this can sometimes come across as downright flirtatious, but how you charm your own customers is entirely down to you.

I had a couple of pairs of binoculars on sale. They actually belonged to my late father-in-law and as I know he used to love my car boot stories, I felt very pleased to be able to perhaps give his items a story of their own.

I thought it prudent to go online and see if they were actually worth something. One pair didn't really seem to show any value but the other one had identical models for sale online for upwards of £15. As there was no time to put them up online, I decided to bring them with me and look at getting that sort of price for them.

Now as this is your first Car Boot Tale, allow me to lay out the ground rules. In every exchange our customer will be given a three-letter code. The code will give a succinct overview of the customer in general and should serve to put you in the frame as well. At the back of the book is a glossary of all of these codes, unless you're reading this on a digital device, in which case just mash your finger over it for a second and the explanation will become all too clear. Then again, it might not. In which case, I apologise, but it just becomes a major burden to start working out a whole chart full of compatible devices and system requirements for what is, at its core – a book.

So let's introduce our first special guest, known to you all as PFE (Pleasant, Fifties, English):

PFE – "Those are some nice binoculars you have there."

Me – "Thank you, that's very kind of you."

PFE – "Have you had much interest in them?"

Surely the only interest which I would register would be someone actually buying them, in which case they would no longer be here and we would not be having this conversation?

Well that's not strictly true, because I understand this question all too well. It's a negotiating tactic. If I've had no interest, then it would make sense for me to lower my prices in order to close a sale. However, this sort of psychological warfare only really works on much larger and expensive items like cars and houses. When it comes to second hand junk, it all feels just a little excessive. Still, as you'll quickly discover as you read this book, everyone loves to 'have a go'.

Me – "Well, to be honest I've only just put them up for sale today. They belonged to my late father-in-law and he had two pairs so I've kept one to give to my son and the other pair is currently in your hands."

PFE – "What sort of price are you looking for?"

Me – "I was looking for twenty pounds." Now let's get some context. Yes I know that there are people selling them online for £15 but you should also know that there are other people selling them for double that. Plus – and this is an important point – he won't have to pay anything for delivery nor come home after work one evening to discover that they're now waiting for him at the Post Office depot which he won't be able to get to until Saturday morning. What price inconvenience? I'd say about a fiver.

PFE – "Ooohh...can you do any better???"

Me – "Certainly I can. Thirty pounds...oh, you meant better for you? No, not yet I'm afraid."

PFE – "How about fifteen?"

Me – "I tell you what, why don't we say seventeen?" (Sure, you maths wizards will have spotted that I have not attempted to meet him half way at all and you are now, in fact, close to tearing up this book in disgust. If so, two things: First, think about switching to decaf, and second – 50p? Do I really want to haggle over 50p? If I go for £18 he might go for it, but he might counter with £17. He also might counter with £17.50 but the fact is that at this level, people round up or down to the nearest pound.

Therefore, I'm either risking him walking away by asking too much or I 'invest' in his interest to the tune of 50p. That term 'invest' is not an accident, these discounts are the means by which you effectively 'buy' your sales. There's no sense in thinking of figures coming off your profit margin because, and I'm fairly sure the smart ones amongst you will have figured this out – you are not making a profit.

PFE – "Deal."

(Told you)

And a little more space on table becomes available for me to put my best stuff forward. You see? A perfectly pleasant exchange with a very nice man who walked away with a very nice pair of binoculars. I vaguely recall he was arrested four months later on twenty-three counts of voyeurism.

Chapter 3 – This Cost Me £300 Brand New

Some people do boot sales as part of their weekly activity as market traders. These people have bought items to sell and this is how they make their living.

No trader will ever be heard to say, "This cost me three hundred quid brand new," because if it did, it would currently be on sale for at least £450. We are not concerned with these people.

You, like so many other people at this sale, are selling off stuff that no longer has a place in your life. They're the electronic toys superseded by mobile phones. They are the toys for a five-year-old who just turned ten. They're the DVDs of box sets and movies that you've long since archived on a hard drive somewhere, never to actually be watched again.

Indeed, collectively the contents of your boot could well have cost you hundreds or even thousands of pounds, but think about it – what are they worth now?

To you, they're worth nothing. The sentimental items have been put into long-term storage - box in loft, furthest from ladder, to be looked at every time you're doing inventory for another sale and AT NO OTHER TIME EVER SO JUST HOW SENTIMENTAL ARE THEY?????

Now that is a whole other can of worms. If you are living with any more than zero people, you're going to have to check on the value of every single thing. Your five-year-old daughter may have not played with that doll since she was six months old but if she discovers that it was removed without her say so, then you are, quite possibly, the most evil person alive and some may even question your right to be a parent.

And, to be fair, it's not just children. Your partner may well have a similar, completely nonsensical (i.e. pointless) reason for holding onto whatever is taking up valuable loft space and it's just so much easier to accept and respect it than risk having that thing you did at a party in 1997 being brought up all over again.

And therapy is expensive, so seriously – just leave it.

Anyway, let's talk about the value of the stuff that is finally permitted to leave the sanctity of the loft and venture forth into the big wide world. Its grand total is...£50. Yup – short drum roll for a small amount of money.

This of course, is going to require a lot more explanation.

You're looking at spending around 7 hours in the field, assuming you arrived at around 5am and pack up at noon.

Your pitch will cost you £13. The journey will be fairly short so let's not bother talking about petrol. Now you may well have incurred other expenses such as a new table, but if we assume that you didn't, if you can turnover £63 then you're looking at £9 per hour. That's better than a lot of people make for actually working, and you're just sitting in a field watching the world go by – pretty sweet arrangement!

So we take our £9, multiply that by 7 and subtract our entry fee, and there's your £50. What this means is that, so long as you can clear £50 in one morning, you will have been able to achieve your primary goal, and that was to get rid of stuff.

Granted, even making a £10 profit is a positive result, but you might not feel the same way when you count up that tenner and realise that it took you seven hours to make it – only you can decide what your time is worth. Even then, it's not really a profit at all, as you are selling off stuff at a fraction of the price you originally paid for it. The sad fact of car boot sales is that you are actually making massive losses, but don't despair – just remember the mantra:

These people are paying me to clean my house.

And once you remember that, you'll quickly realise that even that £10 is a bonus.

Now if your stock looks like it's going to not make you that £50, then you should seriously think about finding out if a friend or relative is doing a sale and ask if they can try and get rid of your stuff for you. You'd actually being doing them a favour too – as a stall with more stuff on it tends to attract more customers. I would not recommend offering to give them a percentage of what they get for you because frankly, it's a major pain in the backside to keep track of who sold what to whom. Just some to a straightforward arrangement and walk away (you don't want things kicking off when you see them again at Christmas, not after last year. You know Aunt Jean never really recovered from that.)

Does this mean you should let someone buy your unwanted *The Lord of the Rings* special edition DVD box set for 50p? Of course not. People are going to make stupid offers, but you'll very quickly start to spot the genuine customers from the tyre kickers. However, unless their offer is truly offensive (and trust me, many of them will be) then start the negotiation and get rid of that stuff.

It may well be that you enjoy the whole adventure of car booting so much that you're not bothered if something takes weeks to sell and you're happy to just keep coming back but...really?...Really though?

Last year I set out with one goal in mind – to come back with an empty boot. Whatever didn't sell would be separated into two piles: charity shop and local dump.

I made £130 at the boot sale, dropped off a box at Cancer Research, drove to the local recycling centre to throw out another box and then drove my empty boot home.

It was the first time I had achieved this in my many years of car booting and I put it down to one simple trick: that everything really did have to go. I would negotiate with people's silly offers and would get the stuff gone, because the item that did cost me £300 eight years ago, was now only worth what the person in front of me was prepared to pay for it.

You need to let go of how much these items cost you when they were new – your buyers don't care. Here, I'll demonstrate:

The buyer here will be categorised as OAL, which stands for Optimistic African Lady. I toyed with the idea of Optimistic Nigerian Lady, but then I realised that I never actually asked her where she was from, and was really only able to use her accent, colour and dress code to a continent, rather than a specific country.

I get the sense that I may have to dedicate an entire chapter to how unbelievably difficult it is not to stereotype your customers. Some may well take offence, seeing me as someone suggesting that all people from any given culture all think, feel and behave the same way.

But sometimes you just get these people...

OAL – "This a fridge?"

OK, hold on, before you start dialling the number for the racist police, please understand that I am trying to portray a character here for you. Her use of language is as intrinsic to the narrative as describing the colour of her dress (it was bright yellow – seriously bright yellow – like looking at a canary flying into the surface of the sun). In order to truly invite you into the scene, my words will have to convey a dialect which is often foreign, and I make no apology for that, because even though these people are real, these people are also characters. Oh, and if you're listening to the audiobook of this, I'm sorry if my African voice does go a little "Nelson Mandela" from time to time.

Me – "Yes, that's right – a mini fridge."

OAL – "How much you want?"

Context Alert – This was part of the house clearance of my late father-in-law's house. It had a shelf missing but aside from that, was in pretty good condition. I decided that an asking price of £7 was reasonable.

Me – "Seven pounds for that."

OAL – "Take five."

Me – Great song, but not overly relevant, or was she perhaps suggesting I took a break? "I'm sorry, but I've literally only just set up and the whole sale isn't officially open yet."

Whilst most boot sales allow people in for free from around 8am, buyers can pay a fee to get in earlier, and many will actually be there before you, lying in wait like a pack of hungry wolves, armed with nothing more than a small selection of pound coins, a wide-eyed sense of ambition, and a large case in which to bring home their kill.

OAL – "Come on, I will give you five." (No, I resisted that joke thank you – come on, we're better than that.)

Me – "It's just a little too early for me to want to bring the price down."

OAL – "Put it aside for me and if you don't sell it, I will give you five."

Me – "Sorry? You want me to take it off the table, so that no one else can see it, and then if I don't sell it by the time you come back, you'll pay me five pounds?"

OAL – "Yes."

Me – "So, just to be clear, and I apologise if I'm repeating myself – I remove it from the items that I have for sale. I wait until you come back and then, because nobody else had the magical foresight to buy an item they couldn't see, you take it from me at a reduced price?"

OAL – "Yes."

Me – "And you can't think of any reason why I might find your proposal ridiculous?"

OAL – "It is a good price, five pounds."

Me – "Tell you what. You pay me five pounds. I'll keep it on the stand and if anyone buys it for seven pounds whilst you're not here, I'll sell it to them and then when you come back I'll give you back your five pounds. If not, then the fridge is all yours."

OAL – (starts laughing and shaking her head) "No no no no no no no no no, I'm not going to do that."

Me – "OK, how about this. You pay seven pounds now and take the fridge, and then if anyone else tries to buy it and doesn't pay more than five pounds, I'll give you two pounds back when you come back later."

OAL – (laughter has now given way to confusion, which is exactly what I was going for.)

Me – "Come on, that's a deal. You get the price you want to pay and I get to sell the fridge."

At this point, OAL starts to do the 'hand waving and walking away' thing and is gone.

About an hour later, a young couple politely asked me if I was prepared to accept £5 and I promptly did. An hour after that, OAL came back and was utterly cross that I had sold the fridge to anyone but her. I felt so guilty I sat down and had a Snickers. And a snicker too, so that works on a number of levels.

Chapter 4 – An Understanding Partner

If you're anything like me, your body clock regularly does this weird thing of waking you up just 5 minutes before your alarm was meant to go off, especially if the alarm in question is set at a socially unacceptable hour. You know – a time which really should only be experienced when you're about to fly off on your holidays – otherwise, leave me alone.

Such a wonderful gift (or curse – depends how you look at it) means that you can quietly switch your alarm off and sneak away undetected. However, for normal people – your alarm is going to wake up your partner. Therefore, as a dutiful husband and one who is about to score some major brownie points with the ladies, I choose to sleep on the couch the night before a very early start (awwwwww – bless him).

For those whose couches simply won't do - lay out your clothes in another room before you go to bed and go and get dressed there, and for God's sake, pick up some flowers on the way home!

Now you may well have loaded up the boot of your car the night, or indeed several days before. However, there is a good chance that both your back seat, and probably passenger seat, are about to be filled up with stuff. The sensible thing to do here is to have that stuff waiting in the hallway, and to allow yourself an extra 15 minutes to load them into the car.

Now I know what you're thinking: "Why not just put everything into the car the night before? That way I can wake up later and just go." A reasonable question, apart from the small issue of security. Leaving anything visible within a car is a recipe for disaster, so don't do it. Unless, of course, you have a garage. Not only that, but a garage in which you actually keep your car. The builders of my house clearly had the best of intentions, just as long as the family car was a Reliant Robin. If you can fit your car in there and also choose to do so, then make sure you have a good rummage around in there too because you're bound to find a few more things that you can sell.

The bolder amongst you may well be thinking, "Well who's going to break into a car for a load of old junk at three in the morning?" Well I don't know you, or indeed where you live, but some of you may well live in a neighbourhood where some toe rag will smash your back window just to get to the half-eaten packet of Fruit Pastilles that you left on the passenger seat. Not to mention that – even though you're the victim here – having your car alarm go off in a residential area in the middle of the might will have you regarded by your neighbours as worse than the love child of Adolf Hitler and Donald Trump!

Better safe than sorry.

Chapter 5 – Dealing with Traders

Getting your stuff together in categories is particularly useful when it comes to dealing with traders. It helps you do business quickly, and also gets these people away from you as fast as human decency will allow.

From what I can ascertain, market traders are, in fact, vampires. No, I'm not saying that they are a horde of blood-sucking monsters – I'm talking about the fact these people will already be waiting for you when you arrive and will act quickly – often not even waiting for you to be out of your car, before they ask you for certain things. All clearly, so they make it back home before the sun rises.

Now as horrible as this sounds, it's actually rather cool, and the reason is, is that these trader vampires all follow the same pattern, meaning that they're all after similar stock.

Good news – I've done your research for you, and the list is pretty short. It is – in no particular order:

Mobile phones
Vinyl records
Electronics
Jewellery

More recently there has been an increase in the number of people asking for trainers. I personally didn't understand the fascination but online research shows me that it can prove to be a very profitable business if you truly know your market and have an eye for rare pieces. In many ways, it's a lot like finding a piece of fine art, except they're shoes. I know, even when I type it, it feels a little ridiculous – I wear my trainers, and then when they're no longer comfortable, I throw them away.

Then I'd like to think that if I weren't the sort of bloke who happily shops in Primark and Lidl as well as John Lewis and Selfridges, that this book may never have been written. It's a world seen not so much through rose-tinted glasses, as through glasses which make everything look...well, how they would to a cynical middle-aged git.

Now if you have any of these items, make sure that you pack them separately to everything else, ideally one box for each group and have a smaller box for jewellery.

Plus, when you are loading up your car, make sure that smaller box travels up front with you but also that those other boxes are within easy reach. These buyers are not known for their patience, and if they're made to stand there whilst you take 12 other boxes out first, then they won't hang around for long. Remember – the sun is rising, they have to be quick.

So quick in fact, that even their speech patterns are abbreviated and rushed. Whereas a normal mortal human may ask, "Good morning. I've come here today in hopes of securing one, or indeed, a small quantity of mobile phones. Would you, perchance, have any which you would consider selling to me?"
"Any mobile?" is more likely what you're going to hear. And remember, you won't hear it all that clearly, because they will not have even waited for you stop the engine and get out of the car.

Now your first reaction, and an understandable one, will be to celebrate the fact that you've started making money before you've set foot on the cold, damp grass. This, however, would be a mistake. You see, not only are these vampires racing against the sun in order to avoid being reduced to ash – they're also racing against each other, so your patience will give you the upper hand.

Once you're given an offer for the phone, simply ask them to come back in 15 minutes. Now I can assure you that their first response will not be a hearty shrug of the shoulders and an agreeable nod. They will immediately default to telling you that you will not get a better offer and that they cannot wait around all day and blah blah white noise blah blah blah.

If they tell you they're not coming back, then please do try and hold back your tears. These vampires really are like buses, in that their pricing structure is an absolute joke and they also smell a bit funny.

The vinyl collectors and jewellers are a little less abrasive, and we'll come on to them later.

Purely for research purposes, and because the bacon roll van hadn't opened yet,

I once asked one of the mobile phone vampires if he could explain how it all worked to me. I explained that I was writing this book and, well here's how that conversation went:

MTV (Male Trader Vampire. Cool initials, by the way) – "Any mobile phones boss?"

Oh yes, did I mention that a lot of them will call you "boss"? Well, they will, with the promise of a delightful cocktail of "bruv, mate and fam" to follow.

Me – "No mobiles sorry, but can I ask you something?"

MTV – ????? – (No words at this stage, just an expression that a normal person might give if you'd ask them to prove the theory of relativity whilst juggling a set of Mars bars)

Me – "You buy these to sell, right?"

MTV – "Yes boss."

Me – "But you don't sell them here, you go to another market?"

MTV – "No, no, we sell them here."

Me – "But then why would I sell to you at a lower price when I could just wait for the customer that was going to buy it from you at a higher price to come to me, and just sell it to him for that myself?"

MTV begins to shake his head and walk away. I was concerned that I may have bamboozled the poor man, until my neighbouring stall holder remarked that this was a perfectly logical question.

I never did get my answer, but I imagine it's because some buyers will flock to those stands which are known for selling electronics, rather than someone who is merely clearing out their junk. As such, those stall holders can buy from the people selling junk, put a small mark-up on each of them and sell them at a profit.

Actually, now that I think about it, it makes perfect sense, which does beg the question of why the vampire simply didn't want to explain it…then again, the first glimpse of the sun had just popped over the horizon.

Chapter 6 – The Pointless Agreement

There are some traders who have followed the ways of the vampire but are still able to walk around fields in the hours of daylight.

They look like us.

But they are not like us.

They are...changed.

To be fair, many of them work in shops and are perfectly nice people. They come to car boot sales in hopes of spotting a rare trinket that they can restore to its former glory and then sell at a profit in their store, at auction, or indeed at their own car boot sale.

Such a gentleman recently came upon my store after espying a watch. The watch in question was a Breitling for Bentley and has a current value of around £4000.

Well the real one would – I bought mine in Hong Kong about ten years ago for £30. It had been living in a drawer for years and as much as I loved to look at it, I had to accept that I just was not wearing it any more.

Many people asked about it at the stand. Indeed, the vampire traders had all taken a look but were not interested in paying what I wanted – which was £30.

A few people even tried it on and one person joked that it would be funny if it were the real thing. I merely nodded and smiled, safe in the knowledge that such fairy tales of junk being found and worth thousands or millions actually only account for about 1 out of every 500 million people in the world, so whilst it pays to be optimistic, you might want to take a closer look at your odds.

And then this happened. Customer shall be given the code VIT – Vampire in Training:

VIT – "That's a nice watch you have there."

Me – "Thanks very much. I was torn whether or not I wanted to sell it, but I just don't wear it enough any more."

VIT – "Any interest?"

Me – "Well you know these things, people ask the price, some might come back, some might not. Right now it's still here and yours if you'd like it." Now it's worth pointing out that a strange metamorphosis had occurred on my part. I consider myself a fairly straight down the line, middle class individual. I like going to markets, but I also enjoy the occasional jaunt around the Selfridges Food Hall.

However, the VIT had a bit more of a blue-collar approach, and as the conversation continued, my own voice and demeanour descended to the point where I could have quite easily broken into a chorus of "Consider Yourself".

VIT – "How much you looking for?"

Me – "Well it's up on eBay right now and I'm really hoping to get thirty quid for it." Cor blimey guv'nor, strike a light.

VIT starts to chuckle to himself. And it's that 'knowing chuckle' that suggests that my price is ridiculous.

VIT – "Thirty you say? That's what I'd charge for it."

Me – (Leaving a pregnant pause to consider my response) "Then we agree." Knowing that our discourse was about to come to a close, I no longer felt the need to act as if I were in a Guy Ritchie movie.

VIT walks away and I'm left baffled at what just happened. It's like this man feels he's at some warehouse that only sell to the trade and here I am, a member of the general public, muscling in on this patch.

Does he seriously think that I am making a point of asking people if they plan to wear the watch or sell it on? After you've paid me my £30 sir, you're more than welcome to insert said watch into any of your own available orifices.

All he did was confirm that I was, in fact, offering the watch at a fair price, and as it was, I sold the watch a little later on that morning to a gentleman on whom it looked good. He paid £25 and that afternoon, found out that this particular replica was a one of a kind, thought to have been made by the Emperor of China when he was a bit bored, and sold it for £4.5million.

Just goes to show you never know.

Chapter 7 – You Owe These People Nothing

Whilst there are many people who will approach your stand purely to play the negotiation game and walk away with nothing but a bruised ego (if you play it the way I taught you), there will be some people that would genuinely like to acquire something that you have on offer.

When it comes to selling off your unwanted electronics, you're bound to generate some interest. Men are like moths to a flame when it comes to shiny metal boxes. Frankly if they're shiny metal boxes with lights on them then those same men are more likely to enjoy an involuntary spasm just below the waist before they walk over.

Selling electronics however, will always attract the same question: "Does it work?" This is where the waters tend to get a little murky, so let's see if we can clean them up.

For me, if a piece of electronic equipment no longer works, I throw it away. Granted, I don't owe these people anything. Some would argue that if you pay £3 for a set of digital cordless phones then having them also work should be considered a bonus.

You can look at another option, and that is to dedicate a section of your stall to all of those electronic items which MAY, but most probably WON'T work. There are plenty of hobbyists that could either try and breathe new life back into that corpse of a VHS player, or they might just want the parts because they've got a team together to enter *Robot Wars* and right now their Killbot VX9000 only comprises a roller skate and a 9-volt battery.

There are those people who will take along a bunch of stuff, completely untested, and allow their punters to take a gamble – after all, if it doesn't work, they've only lost a couple of quid, right?

Sorry, but that just doesn't sit well with me. Some of these people might be buying electronic toys for their children, and just how is that going to look when they put in some fresh batteries and nothing happens? Bad for the child, worse for the parent and you're already far too tired from the 4.30am alarm to start wondering how you can possibly sleep at night, you monster!

The point is that as you are not governed by any legal trading standards authority, the only higher power to which you have to report is your own conscience. That being said, if people want to buy electronics that are guaranteed to work, then there are places that they can shop from. You may be familiar with them – they have roofs, aisles and aisles of products, and an array of staff who generally don't give a toss. Small wonder some people choose to take their chances in a field – oh sure, there's no guarantee that the stuff will actually work, but can you actually put a price on playful banter? All of which leads me – rather neatly, I think we can all agree – to this next tale.

Item for sale is indeed the set of digital cordless phones that I mentioned earlier. They did work fine except one of the handsets lost its charge quite quickly, but I had already solved that issue. To fix it properly would have involved my going to a shop that sells the sort of special-sized rechargeable AA batteries that go in these phones. And no, not all AA batteries are the same size – these ones are fractionally bigger than normal ones which means that, whilst regular AA rechargeable batteries will fit, they won't charge up properly. You see, not just Boot smarts – you get physics thrown in for free!

The cost of these would be £12.99. I didn't see it likely that the phones would sell for more than £15 so I chose to just be up front with the customer.

A tactic which ultimately lead to the sort of exchange about which books are written. So that's handy then.

The customer is being categorised under the code WSV, which stands for World's Smallest Violin.

WSV – "This is telephone?" The lady in question looked to be in her forties and spoke in a pattern which suggested that English was not her first language. It would become quickly apparent, that common sense lagged somewhere behind as well.

Me – "It's actually a set of three telephones, and I have all of the chargers and base units here, so it's a complete set – I've even got the instruction manual for you." Yes, keep instruction manuals – you may never read them yourself but when it comes to selling on, these little booklets are the cherry on a very cheap cake.

WSV – "It's all working?" (Told you)

Me – "It is, although this one does need a new set of batteries and you can get them in Maplin* for about twelve pounds, although there may be some other places you can get them for less."
* When I met this lady, Maplin was a thriving high street chain. Now – well, not so much.

WSV – "But is working?"

Me – "Absolutely. In fact if you're the sort of person that leaves your phone in the cradle between calls, you might not even want to bother with the battery."

WSV – "I don't know."

Me – "I understand. No pressure, what is it that you don't know about?"

WSV – "Well I've bought three now from car boot and when I go home they not working."

Time freezes at this point for me to enjoy a small internal rant. Well, it's not so much a rant but a question, and one that, if asked out loud, would doubtless cause some offence. Or a round of applause, depending where you were in the proceedings.

Have you heard of shops? You know…shops…where the stuff is new and comes in a box and a warranty in case of problems? There's a very strong chance that if you add up all the money you've spent on broken phones at car boot sales, you could have actually bought a really nice new one from an actual, proper shop.

More than that, why do you people (by which I mean customers – race didn't come into it) think that all of us stall holders are working together under one massive car boot conglomerate? Do you think we all actually get here at 2am, dance around a burning statue of the devil and then discuss our plans for world domination?

"Come forward Brother Paul and pledge your worth to the congregation."

"Blessed be – brothers and sisters of The Boot, and gaze upon the glory that is this twenty-year-old toaster that either burns toast or shorts out an entire cul-de-sac."

"Blessed be Brother Paul, and may good fortune and quite nice weather for this time of year be upon you."

Yes there are people selling shoddy broken crap and I'm afraid you've only got my word for it, but I'm not one of them.

So stop feeding me your sob story, which we all know is just a weak negotiating tactic anyway, and get on with buying this bloody phone whilst I play the World's Smallest Violin.

See? I told you these codes would make sense if you gave them a chance. Best restart time and continue our conversation...

Me – "Well that is bad luck, but I don't really know what else to say. I've been completely up front about a small problem which you might encounter, but beyond that you'd really just have to trust me" (or go to a shop...you know – shops???)

WSV – "OK, how much you want?"

Me – "It's fifteen pounds for that."

WSV – "Oh dear, really I don't want to pay more than five."

Me – "If I may. If someone is prepared to sell you one hundred pounds' worth of telephones for five pounds, then I fear you may be returning home with another broken phone. Now you say you've bought three sets so far, yes?"

WSV – "Yes, three."

Me – "OK, so assuming that you paid five pounds each time there, you've spent fifteen pounds on broken phones, and of course we can't really put a price on the hassle of coming out to a field at dawn on a Sunday morning, can we?"

WSV – (smiles)

Me – "I'm saying you can spend that fifteen pounds right here and right now and leave with a phone which absolutely works. Think about it. You'll never have to look at phones at boot sales again."

WSV – "Will you take ten?"

Me – "Madam, you've just bought yourself a phone."

Sale made, unwanted phones gone, conscience clear, next customer please.

Chapter 8 – Stories Sell

There's a well-known phrase from the play *Glengarry Glen Ross*, as delivered by Alec Baldwin, and it's meant as a mantra to sales people: ABC – Always Be Closing.

Now the mechanics of this statement are a book unto themselves, and if you're looking for a sales training book which will help you to close million dollar deals rather than getting some woman to part with an extra 50p for a knitted sweater, then you've clearly purchased the wrong book.

However, this mantra is clear to see at your average car boot sale – from the buyers using every ounce of flawed logic to knock down a price, to the sellers trying to convince people of stuff which, if you really took the time to think about it, absolutely beggars belief.

In my most recent sale I was situated next to a stall run by a very loud and overbearing woman with an accent that placed her from somewhere in Eastern Europe. I could have asked where she was from, but the way she spoke to people in general made me almost certain that I would rather have been locked in a glass cabinet and made to watch episodes of *Peppa Pig* for an entire week rather than strike up a conversation with her.

She had, on her stand, a lamp. Now even though we can all agree that one man's (or woman's) is indeed another man's (or woman's – oh look, can we just stop all this PC nonsense? If I jump straight back to what came before the brackets that opened this bit, you won't even remember what I was saying. Think so? OK, let's see) treasure, this lamp was, to use a term I picked up from a well-renowned antique dealer – ugly as... let's say 'sin', as there may be children reading.

The lady wanted £15 for this lamp and pointed out to every single person that so much as looked at it, that it was "brand new", and there was even a price tag on there to prove that its original value was £100.

So, let's strip this down, one bit at a time, shall we? Brand new? You have an item worth £100 that you bought and then instantly decided you no longer wanted but, rather than simply taking it back to the original shop, you decide to knock 85% off of the value and sell it in a misty field at 6am on a Saturday? And did I say 85%? Oh wait, it gets better, as when people walk away from the lamp, the lady calls out that they can have it for a tenner.

Brand new? Where's the box? Where's the protective plastic that it would have come in? Now you may be thinking that perhaps she disposed of these, which may well be true – but there's still a price tag on the item in question. Who disposes of all the packaging and yet doesn't remove the price tag? Only two types of people – liars and psychos – either way the game's afoot, and I've already ruled out Colonel Mustard in the library with the candlestick.

She also claims that the main body of this lamp is genuine oak. It may well be – my years of woodworking experience extend no further than balsa – but surely the wood in question is of little consequence when the carpenter clearly downed half a bottle of tequila and then went to town with his chisel.

What was happening here is that the vendor believed that she had something which looked like it had value, and it would have been so much easier to get people to buy into that value if she had used one simple little tool.

A story.

Every single item on your stand has a story. You might not remember all the details, but stories sell items, and the truth is, you probably remember more than you think.

A story is what sets you aside from a shop. Shops sell things, but you are parting with memories, and if something has a powerful memory for you, then that power can be transferred to the next owner, and once that happens, the price of the item becomes secondary to its true value.

Now we're not looking for some Dickensian masterpiece here – just a few choice pieces of information.

Grab one of the items you're planning on selling and see how many of these questions you can answer:

Who used this item the most in your house?
Did you buy it or was it a gift?
Why are you looking to sell it?
Did you have to ask permission from the primary user to sell it?
Did you buy it somewhere interesting, perhaps overseas?
Do you know what similar items are selling for on eBay?
Have you a price in mind?
How long has it been since you used it last?
Is there any reason to hold on to it?
How do you feel about parting with it?

These questions are your items stories – and stories sell. Just look at our lamp example – her claims of the item being "brand new" over and over again just caused me to roll my eyes into the back of my skull and at one point I actually muttered under my breath "No it isn't." I had regarded this person as full of crap, which may or may not have been a fair judgement. Perhaps if she had explained why she was in possession of a brand-new lamp that she could not take back to the shops then perhaps someone may have bought it. Someone with very poor taste, I hasten to add. Really, I cannot over emphasise the sheer aesthetic disaster that was this lamp.

For the record, a nice couple did actually but the glass lampshade, and paid what the lady would have taken for the entire lamp, but they REALLY didn't want it, and so took it apart on the stand, thus turning a fairly unattractive floor standing lamp into a bloody ugly stick with a bulb at the top. Of course, if it is real oak (it isn't) then at least it will float back up when she tries to chuck it in the nearest canal.

Joking aside, please dispose of your monstrosities responsibly.

Chapter 9 – The Magic Hat

By now you will have seen that people will try anything, and I do mean anything, to get you to lower your prices. There are several ways you can respond to this. You can choose to get wound up and tell them to go away. Believe it or not, this is actually the reaction of choice for many a stall holder.

Other people will happily enter into a negotiation, and why not? The car boot sale is not a place where goods are sold at the advertised price. The sellers know it, the buyers know it, so let's all just enjoy a jolly good rally of playful banter and walk away invigorated!

Of course, there is the third group that will write down all of these stupid negotiations and turn them into a book, but those people are just plain weird, so let's not talk about them. However, if you're looking for a wonderful example of an utterly ridiculous attempt at negotiation, then look no further. Well, obviously look a little bit further – why would you just stop reading there?

Long before I thought up acronyms to describe these people, I used simpler terms. This is rather an old story, but I just really like the nickname that I gave him, so I'm not going to change it. In the story, the role of 'dim-witted customer' will be played by "Potato" and to offer you some context (which you really don't need), I was attempting to sell some old beanie hats.

Potato: "What these?" Now, I'm not saying he was a foreign person, let's not get into that, but...well...you know...

Me: "They're beanie hats, and this one has headphones built in, so they're great for when you're out for a run." In truth, not really that great. The headphones are inserted into the hat in such a way that removing them to wash the hat was incredibly difficult. So much so that the first attempt quickly became the last attempt.

Potato: "They work?" Never gets old.

Me: "They do. In fact, you can test them here if you like, I've brought my iPod along."

Testing follows and the reaction on the man's face suggests that he was expecting to hear an audio quality akin to a live concert at the Royal Albert Hall, only to find himself just a little disappointed. Perfectly reasonable when you're being asked to part with a solitary pound – about which, he was about to be.

Potato: "How much you want?"

Me: "Just one pound for those." An absolute steal but come on, it was close to the end of the day, and this hat had been part of my marathon training. Now remember what I said about the washing. Yep – ewwwwwwwwwwwww!

Potato: "I'll give you 50p."

Me: "No, come on – one pound for those is still a very good price. You'd be paying that just for earphones on their own, let alone the hat."

Potato: "Well, I'll give you 50p because it's a bit small."

OK, do you need a minute at this point? Time to gather your thoughts? It's fine, really, I don't mind. When someone sucks all of the logic and reason out of the room, it's perfectly normal in the absence of any weaponry, to just take a moment to regain your composure. Ready? Great, let's jump back in…

Me: "Well I don't imagine paying less for it is going to make it grow any time soon. Or does your head magically shrink when you pay less than the full price for something?"

Potato parts with his pound. As he walked away, his head expanded like a giant balloon and he floated off into the clouds, never to be heard of again. A condition which I am told, can be cured for 50p. Ironic really.

Chapter 10
Thought That Hat was Magic?
Try the Even More Magical Shoe

There's a common negotiation tactic that I hear a number of times at any boot sale at which I work. Now, stay with me here because these can get complex. Let's call our customer NFP, and just for a change, I'm going to let you work out what it stands for.

NFP – "How much for this?" You know what's great about that question, is that I can say it in any accent, be it foreign or domestic, and it works in all of them. I like that – very Zen.

Me – "It's a pound."

NFP – "Not 50p?"

Me – "No."

Now you may well be thinking that what the buyer has done here is automatically attempt to halve the price of the item in question, except that it doesn't appear to work that way. Take a close look at this exchange:

NFP – "How much?"

Me – "Those are two pounds."

NFP – "Not 50p?"

Me – "No."

It's like they've chosen this magical figure and regardless of what item they're holding in their hands, they simply must question why it is I won't sell it to them for 50p.

Do they conduct themselves in this manner in any other negotiation? "Well the vendors have priced the house to sell as they've found what they hope will be their next home, so even though a house like this usually fetches three hundred and fifty thousand they're actually happy to accept offers in the region of three hundred and twenty K."

"Not 50p?"

"Get out."

And so it was that magical negotiation that lead me to create the Magical Shoe scenario. Now first I should explain a little context. I told you at the outset of this book that every single tale in here was real. Whilst writing this book, I had an idea for a funny story, but if I just randomly inserted it somewhere (oo-er, missus) then the whole thing about every story being true would be a lie, and I simply can't do that to you.

Therefore, I set about crafting a set of responses in the hopes that just one buyer might actually play along. I'm delighted to say that he did. All of this really did happen.

The item in question was a pair of shoes. They belonged to my daughter, who was about to turn 6, and like all children that age, their shoes are usually too small for them within 48 seconds of leaving the shoe shop, stepping onto the pavement and invalidating any warranty.

Like all shoes at a car boot sale, set your price low and then just stick to it. Bear in mind that if you are selling shoes at a boot sale, don't bring along pairs which are on their last legs (see what I did there). If they're in a shocking state of repair, then you're better off throwing them away. No one is likely to buy them and they'll be taking up valuable space in your boot which could otherwise be taken up by that collection of Fabergé eggs that you're looking to flog.

Our player enters from stage left. Or is it right? It's so easy to get these mixed up when you're performing 'in the round', so to speak.

NFP – "How much you want for the shoes?"

Me – "Those are just a pound."

NFP – And I think we all know what's coming here, don't we? No? Seriously? You still need me to spell it out? OK then… "Not 50p?"

Me – Let us freeze frame on this for a second, which is odd, because when I freeze frame at car boot sales in my mind, it's always a sort of VHS freeze frame. You know the picture is clear enough, but there's some thin white line that wobbles on the bottom of the screen. Perhaps it's something to do with my being surrounded by second hand junk.

The freeze frame is there, in this case, for me to enjoy one solitary thought: "YEEEESSSSS!!!!!!!! I can do the Magical Shoe bit and put it in the book."

OK, hit the play button on the remote. The remote. Oh come on I left it on the coffee table. What do you mean you can't see it? Well just go over to the machine and play it then. Fine, I'll do it.

Me – "Well you can give me 50p, but that means you're only walking away with one shoe. Did you want the left or the right?"

NFP – A playful chap who clearly enjoys the banter. "OK, I will take the left one." This is fantastic! I mean this bloke has not even been given the script but he is literally playing out the sketch in my mind, right in front of me. You couldn't make it up. Well you could, because I did, but here we are.

Me – "Interesting. Actually, you're doing me a favour there."

NFP – "How?"

Me – "Well, I'm sure you know that most people selling shoes at car boot sales tend to sell them in pairs. A single shoe would be quite the rare find; The Holy Grail of Shoes – if you will. Just imagine – here you are, walking around this market in the hopes of buying one solitary shoe and yet, everywhere you go, all these people – these leeches – are forcing you to buy twice the number of shoes that you actually want. It's downright insensitive if you ask me."

NFP – "But…"

Me – "But you sir, are clearly someone with a keen eye. In all your travels for this mystical item, fate has brought you here, to me, on this blessed day. You've managed to find the legend of the solitary shoe for only 50p. Clearly, I set the price way too low, but I had no way of knowing you would be here. Well, that's my mistake and I'm sure I'll come to terms with it in time, sir. But now I am faced with an even greater quest – what to do with the other shoe?

Now it is truly a single item, its equal being sold to your good self, and so I will immediately raise the price. I think two pounds is more than fair, although, and I know I may regret this, I could let you have it at a reduced rate. Would you take it off my hands for a pound? Actually, no, don't even answer that, I already know what you're going to say – why don't we say 50p?"

NFP – "So still a pound for the pair then? OK."

He paid his money and took his shoes.

Chapter 11 – Negotiation

I LOVE negotiating, and when you're dealing in small sums of money, it really is just one big game, and one which should never be taken seriously. Any references to Monty Python's *Life of Brian* are meant by way of an homage. This is because the "We're supposed to haggle" scene is just one in a multitude of sheer comedic genius.

In the world of the car boot – haggling is practically mandatory. Sadly, there are some people who take it just a little too far and actually try and argue down the price of a bacon roll and a cup of tea from the snack van. If you're not too sure about car boot protocol, let me tell you that that's just not cool.

But this is about you as a seller, and firstly, we need to talk about your valuation of your stuff.

A wise man once told me that things are only worth what people are prepared to pay for them. That's very true, most people need a starting figure to help start the process. When someone asks you the price of something, the response of "Make me an offer," simply doesn't work. Many of them will just put it back down and walk off, which has always struck me as weird.

No, seriously, can we talk about that for a second? You pick something up, which means it is of interest to you. You ask the merchant (sure, let's go with merchant for this bit) how much it is and he hands you a golden ticket. He has literally just told you to name your price. You could be walking away with a brand-new Blu-ray player for 20p but instead, you shake your head, put it down and walk away.

What the actual heck? (Look, my kids might read this.) It happens to me every single sale I go to and I still just cannot understand it. I'm sure some smarter observer of anthropology might suggest that we all stem from a tribal culture where it was important that a leader was asserted quickly. The strongest and most aggressive would battle for this position until one was made the clear leader, whilst the less aggressive were happy to assume the role of a follower.

Evolve us through several million years and two of the less aggressive members of the tribe are faced with a power struggle. One of them has picked up the rock but doesn't want to declare his dominance for fear that he will be challenged by the other larger and hairier members of the tribe. The other one is happy to part with the rock but does not want to be thought of as weak by the first, and so proposes a trade through a series of grunts and bizarre hand gestures.

And so, we arrive at an impasse. The first warrior wants the rock, the second warrior want to part with the rock, but regrettably, nobody gets the rock, and the first warrior retreats to his cave.

Yes indeed, some smarter observer might think that. They may even publish a paper on it, further explaining that the rock in question was a vintage cake stand and the cave in question was the next stall where some lady had a selection of buttons available.

To those who share my intellectual plane, let's just agree that some people are prats.

Chapter 12 – The Diamonds

As I've mentioned before, anyone choosing to set up their stall early enough will first be met by traders. These people will buy your junk, take it somewhere else and then sell it at a profit.

And why not? Whilst many of us are simply looking to claim an extra four square feet in our loft to store stuff which will almost certainly be in next year's car boot sale, many people there are actually making a living, although given that they will buy something from you for four pounds in order to go and sell it for six, one does have to wonder just how good a living it is. Sure, the economists amongst you will observe that he is enjoying a margin of just under 33%, whereas the rest of us would happily trade in the chance to make £2 for an extra four hours in bed on a Sunday morning.

The traders typically want electronics and mobile phones. Others will ask about vinyl, but the other group – well they are just precious. These people want jewellery. And we are not talking shopping centre concession stand jewellery. Oh no. These people came to play.

Enter the muppet, who in this story will be played by LBT – Loud, Big Teeth. Originally, I was going to refer to him as Wildly Optimistic Gentleman but I realised that the acronym could get me into quite a lot of trouble.

LBT: "GOOD MORNING MY FRIEND!" Yes, I am using all caps to indicate the level of enthusiasm being shown by this man. The only thing louder than his voice was the whiteness of his smile.

Me: "Good morning." I'm not your friend. I like to think of myself as fairly approachable, but to be fair, I'd need an awful lot more Red Bull/coffee/class A narcotics to get anywhere close to reflecting his charmingly jolly persona. I say charming, really, it's more instantly jarring.

LBT: "Any je*&^GER%FSER?" Not a typo – I genuinely could not understand the noise he had just let fall out of his mouth.

Me: "Sorry, what was that?"

LBT: "Any F*8K£#¢∞? jewellery?" Again, not replacing a swear word here, he clearly listed some other items first, but I believe it would take the translation powers of the TARDIS to understand what he was going on about.

Me: "Oh jewellery. Sorry but my ears were still ringing from your initial greeting. I've got a couple of watches if you're interested. Not exactly highbrow but you're welcome to have a look. What sort of jewellery are you after?"

LBT: "Costume jewellery, you know...diamonds..."

OK, hold on a second. Yep. The man has just asked a bloke unloading the boot of a Seat Toledo at 6am on a Sunday in Watford if he has any diamonds on him.

Me: "Did you just say diamonds?"

LBT: "Yeah. You never know, you might get lucky."

Me: "Does that happen a lot then? People unknowingly bring thousands of pounds worth of diamonds to car boot sales?"

I mean sure, we've all read the stories of the little old lady who turns up with a vase to Sotheby's and walks out with £8 million which she then leaves to the local cat home, but this is the stuff of tabloid newspapers and Disney movies. In a car boot sale in Watford, I'd say the odds are firmly against you.

At which point LBT walks away and three other people setting up their own stalls come over to tell me that they heard our exchange and thought that the whole thing was ridiculous, but hilarious at the same time. So that was a great start to the day, and ironic really, because the Van Gogh I had on the passenger seat is still up for grabs.

Chapter 13 – The Car Boot Supermarket

It's fair to say that any given car boot sale will allow you to enjoy the full spectrum of human behaviour – from the sharp negotiator with a keen mathematical mind, through to the sorry chancer who could not negotiate his way out of a paper bag.

These people do mean well, but they ultimately want to play the game, which gives you one of two choices: number one – you can politely tell them to go away. In truth, I've seen many a stall holder choose to be a lot less polite. Once there's only an hour left to go before packing up and someone tries to haggle over 50p for a saucepan, there are many market traders who will just flat out lose it and tell these people just what they can do with their crappy offers.

I can totally relate to why people might choose to do this – their time, and indeed their sanity is worth more to them than putting up with one more moron. Trouble is that they've clearly forgotten where they are – in a field surrounded by morons – which leads us to choice number two: play the game as well.

Remember that in any negotiation, the goal is to win. Just remember that for you, a win is someone giving you money to take away your junk. For the buyer, the win is getting you down to the lowest price they can. Do you see how you already have the upper hand? If they really held out, you could let the stuff go for a penny and you would have still won the game. The important thing is not to let them know that.

The real fun comes with their tactics, and I love these people for trying. Now in this case, the item in question was a selfie stick – an unwanted gift, offered to us by way of an apology when the company's customer service was a little below par. We got some other things too, because, let's be honest, just giving someone a selfie stick to say sorry is tantamount to slapping them in the face with a nearby pineapple.

Let's us refer to this buyer with the code JAP, which stands for 'Just a plank', which is the opinion I quickly formed of him.

JAP – "What is this?"

Me – "It's a selfie stick – brand new there, still in the box – never been used." True story – the company actually gave me and my wife one stick each. The second is being used to document some of the stories for the video version of this book.

JAP – "How much you want?" Could be read as a little rude and direct, but really that's just a by-product of English not being his first language. As I believe I have already mentioned, his first language is Plank.

Me – "It's five pounds."

JAP – "The man over there has one for three pounds."

AAAARRRGGGHHHH!!! I HATE this one, because I come across it not just at boot sales, but pretty much everywhere, and my answer is always the same:

Me – "OK, well you should probably go and buy that then." Seriously, I don't care what someone else is selling it for. Some other shop is selling it for £10, so what? No matter how cheap a product or service is, there's always someone offering to do it for less.

The trouble is that when people employ this tactic, they're immediately shooting themselves in the foot. They are confessing that there is a reason why they simply haven't bought the item from the other place. Now of course, they don't know the other person's stuff is cheaper until they've seen yours, but now they know both prices, why not head straight back to the other stall?

Think about it – if they have an identical item that's cheaper, why would you not just buy it? Oh sure, you're telling me in hopes that I will lower my price to match but I am not some high street chain store with a price-matching policy and a group of shareholders to whom I need to answer. I'm a bloke in a field with a selfie stick that I no longer want. You're more than welcome to spend the rest of your day trying to save that all important £2 sir, and quite frankly I wish you would set off on that quest forthwith. Of course, this entire response is held in, boring a hole in the lining of my stomach.

JAP – "Can you do it for three pounds?"

Me – "No, I'm sorry – it's brand new, it's five pounds for that."

JAP – "But his is three."

Ah yes, the unbreakable loop negotiation, whereby the buyer believes that saying the exact same thing as the thing they said ten seconds ago, now has so much more bearing on the case.

Me – "Yes, I understand that, and you find yourself in an enviable position, because if you only want to pay three pounds for a selfie stick, then you already know where to go." Here's a clue for you Plank – it's 'away from here'.

JAP – "Well what's the difference between yours and his?"

It's OK – take a moment. Just breathe. At this stage, any psychotic tendencies you feel towards this buyer are completely justified. Sadly it's only 7.30 in the morning, so drink, drugs or a combination of the two are not really an option. You're going to have to see this one through – just put down the sharp object.

Me – "I don't really know how you would expect me to know the answer to that. I didn't make a point of researching my competitors before I unloaded the car. In my defence, I'm fairly sure the other guy would offer you a similar response."

JAP then proceeded to test the item, decided that it was not for him, and left without the stick in question, although he did come dangerously close to having me insert it somewhere for him, at which point I would have let him keep it for free.

Chapter 14 – The Power of Your Mobile

To truly utilise this power, you will need three things:

An item on your stand which is worth more than £20.
A mobile phone with a data connection.
A Facebook account.

As you arrive and start unloading your stuff, you're going to come across certain items that you had almost completely forgotten about. You packed them neatly into a box months ago, waiting for the weather to become pleasant, and now here they are, ready to be flogged.

The trouble with car boot sales is that more expensive items can be much more difficult to sell – especially to those people who have shown up with 75p in 2p pieces and a wildly deluded sense of ambition.

These days it's easier to shift such things online, but just in case you forgot, here's what you do. Take a photo of the item and immediately post it on Facebook Marketplace. It's free, immediate and best of all – location based.

But here's the trick. Advertise it for more than you're willing to accept. This might seem obvious, but the fact is that Facebook Marketplace works exactly the same way as a car boot sale – people make offers and you either accept or decline.

If someone starts expressing a lot of interest in the item in question, tell them that it is for sale online and show them the advert. They'll see that you're serious about parting with it and may well make you a reasonable offer. Once again, if it's unreasonable, you can simply decline, telling them that you've had plenty of people asking about it online but you figured you might as well bring it to the sale, just in case it could be sold quickly.

By having your phone handy, you can easily show them the listing, which creates a feeling from the buyer's perspective that you're not simply making up a price on the spot or are open to offers, but that you are a serious seller who's pitched your stall in both the physical and virtual world. One way or another, that item is going to sell, and there's a good chance you'll be pleasantly surprised to sell it for more than you'd originally hoped.

Chapter 15 – Trust Issues

Now let me make one thing abundantly clear before you read any further. This section is not to cast a shadow over your moral fibre. I am going to assume that you are an honest and decent individual who will gladly help little old ladies across the street and stop following any friends on social media who start talking about *Love Island* or Brexit. Yes indeed – you're my kind of people, and therefore, I trust you.

But in the minds of your customers, you are a thieving con artist who will put up his own grandmother in part exchange for a packet of Monster Munch.

Sadly, market traders get a bad rap. Low prices, eclectic stock and the ability to pick up the shop and disappear cause a lot of customers to suspect that they're up to no good, and this mistrust is easily transferred into the world of the car boot sale.

As I've mentioned before, people will assume that your electronics don't work, that your antiques are all fake and that the dress you want £1.50 for is barely even worth £1.25. Seriously, how do you sleep at night, you monster?

So what's the solution? Well if anyone is buying an expensive gadget from you, you could offer them your phone number. That way, if there are any problems, you will be happy to discuss them. The trouble is – and frankly if you need me to point this out at this stage then I suggest you start reading this book again from the beginning – there are a lot of very odd people out there, and giving your phone number to them could be a recipe for disaster.

Besides, what guarantee does a mobile number give them anyway? As soon as someone becomes a pest you'd block their number and that would be the end of it, so why even bother offering it up?

The point of a car boot transaction is that it all works under the glorious banner of Caveat Emptor, or for anyone who didn't study Latin (most of us) that means Buyer Beware.

Who's going to car boot sales to buy expensive gadgets anyway? By all means put them out on display and offer your email address up to anyone displaying a little bit of doubt, but otherwise, let these people assume the risk. Granted, there are a lot of people selling a lot of broken crap under the premise that it all works fine, but take some comfort in the fact that you are not one of them. Take a moment of positive self-reflection, reward yourself with a smile and a custard cream, and then go on about your day.

That said, when it comes to a lack of trust, some people will stretch it to breaking point, which naturally leads me on to this delightful anecdote. The item in question was a mini snooker table. When I say mini, this thing was a toy measuring about eight inches long and was an unwanted gift from one of those Scandinavian high street stores which seem to sell just a little bit of everything whilst simultaneously being utterly pointless.

The toy had never been opened. The box was sealed and shrink-wrapped and there was a picture of the toy on the box, just so that children and the mentally deficient could be sure they knew what they were getting.

Or so you would like to think.

Customer enters stage left and shall be referred to as WFM, which stands for Words Fail Me.

WFM picks up the box and begins to study it in great detail. She puts it back down again and continues casting her eye over my stall. Minutes pass and she once again picks up the box. I engage in eye contact and a welcoming smile. WFM continues to study the box, clearly hoping that it is some lost artefact that Indiana Jones must have stolen back from the Nazis, but still no words are exchanged.

Eventually, she draws breath, and one can only imagine the PhD dissertation question that her brain has finally sent down to her mouth. "How much is it?" No – too obvious. "Is this brand new?" Reasonable but again, not this time. So, ready, here we go, here comes the opening gambit to another successful sale...

WFM – "Is this this?"

Me – "I'm sorry?" To be clear, I'm not sorry, I'm dumbfounded. She is pointing to the picture of the item on a sealed box and is asking if the picture refers to the contents. Now I'm no marketing expert, but in my experience, most manufacturers, if choosing to use any imagery at all, will default to putting an image of the actual product on the box. Rarely, if ever, have I opened a box with a picture of a toy car on it and been pleasantly surprised to have been presented with a fondue set and £20,000 in holiday vouchers.

Who does this person think she's dealing with here – Willy frickin' Wonka? There's no golden ticket sweetheart, this is very much a Ronseal moment for you, in that it does exactly what it says on the tin, or in this case, the box!

Naturally, this thought process did not take place in real time, as that would have been rude. Hence my carefully constructed reply:

Me – "Yes."

WFM puts the box down and walks away, clearly disappointed that the whole car boot experience was not more akin to some sort of lucky dip, where you think you're buying a Barbie doll with an eyelash missing for 50p, but are in fact about to drive away in a brand-new Bentley.

Better luck next time.

Chapter 16 – I'm Leaving Now

No matter how bizarre someone's negotiating position is, I can always find a little glimpse of logic on their part which explains the whole thing away.

Usually.

But not always.

The item in question was a large cuddly toy koala that made cute little noises, blinked its huge eyes, drank from a bottle, ate from a giant eucalyptus leaf and was a source of amusement and amazement to my four-year-old daughter.

For about an hour. After which this large robotic toy was not so much cute as it was annoying and large. It also depreciated faster than a timeshare next to a newly-discovered volcano, so it had to go.

Online research had suggested that a figure between £15 and £20 would be reasonable for it, so I put it online for £20 and then gave it pride of place on the stand. After all, to the uninitiated, this thing was amazing. They had yet to learn the horror of trying to find the off switch nestled under a very ill-fitting Velcro strap, or the battery compartment with screws so small that only a skilled neurosurgeon would dare attempt to replace the batteries without losing her mind.

A lady approaches. It's fairly early in the day, so there's really no reason for me to consider lowering my price, aside from the desperate need to remove this Stephen King novel of a toy from my life.

The lady will be referred to as ILN. The reasons won't be immediately obvious, unless you pay attention to the sub headings of these stories – in which case I've already given you the answer:

ILN – "Ooh I've seen these. They're great, aren't they?"

Me – "Yes." Oh don't judge me! Just because I don't think it's great doesn't mean that someone else won't – it's subjective.

ILN – "How much are you asking for it?"

Me – "Well I have it online for twenty pounds at the moment. Still early days but I'm fairly certain it'll be gone by the end of the day."

ILN – "OK I'll come back later."

This is a response which rarely, if ever, turns out to be true.

Then again, I did say 'rarely', because lo and behold, some ninety minutes later, she did indeed return.

ILN – "Not sold it yet then?" Her powers of observation floor me. Clearly there is no outsmarting my intellectual superior. I must proceed with caution.

Me – "Yes I have. I actually sold it 1500 times in the last hour. People just handed me their money and then asked me to keep it here and yet they never came back. To be honest with you, after I'd made the first ten thousand I thought about calling it a day, but they just kept on coming."

I didn't actually say any of those things, but at this stage, you probably wouldn't have put it past me, would you?

Me – "No, not yet."

ILN – "Will you take ten for it?"

Me – "Why don't we split the difference and call it fifteen?"

ILN – "Well I've only got ten and I'm leaving now."

OK hang on. I get the first bit. If you've genuinely only got £10 left on you then there's really very little harm in trying that tactic. It's honest and straightforward and I actually don't mind it. Sure, in other walks of life such tactics are completely ineffective, but this isn't high finance – it's a car boot sale and therefore anything goes.

But it's the second bit which threw me: "I'm leaving now." As if to suggest that hers is the only money in the field and once it's gone, it's gone. Did she think I was sat there counting the moments until she returned? More importantly, if money is a little tight, perhaps the best thing to do is not buy this item for any amount at all. Oh sure, £10 might feel like a bargain now, but I can assure you that your buyer's remorse will have flooded your system before tea time.

Now, it would have been so easy for me to say that she walked away without the bear with her purse still that £10 heavier. But I took one long look at this now truly annoying stealer of cupboard space and agreed to part with it for the princely sum of £10, so you could argue that ILN had won this round. However, I knew what she had really just paid £10 for – to inherit one of my personal demons and care for it for just as long as she could stand before confining it to either a skip or another car boot sale, thus continuing the cycle of pure evil mwah ha ha ha ha…

You may not be able to put a price on peace of mind, but £5 buys you some much needed storage space in your cupboards, not to mention no longer having to resist shouting, "Shut that bloody bear up," to a six-year-old girl, so take the money and run!

And yes, I am aware that a Koala is not technically a bear, thank you very much.

Chapter 17 – The Truth Doesn't Hurt

Back when I had a 'proper job', I worked in the promotional merchandise industry and had a monthly column in their most popular magazine. Once a month I would attempt to provide some insight into how we, as sales people, could all do a better job.

What the reader ended up with was a rant about how some people really should be removed from the general populace and used as some sort of industrial fertiliser.

One gripe with which I always had a problem was the polite liars, and yes, of course, you get them in every walk of life, including car boot sales.

Sales people get to deal with a lot of polite liars. They're the people that ask you to send an email to introduce your company, or perhaps to send some literature in the post – all of which we know, they will never read.

These people are just being polite. After all, it's just plain nasty to tell someone that you have no interest in working with them. Funny how we don't seem to feel the same way towards people calling us with PPI and accident claims, but that's a whole other story.

The truth is that these people are, in fact, evil. They are time-sucking leeches and they need to be stopped, by any means necessary. And it's not just time that they want to suck out of you – it's money. Sending out literature that will be used to line dustbins and bird cages costs money.

But forget about time and money, as if that weren't bad enough. These people actually rob you of your hope. They let you feel, even just for a fleeting moment, that you may be blessed with the opportunity to work with them, and perhaps even make enough money to buy that vintage collection of Corn Flake packets that you saw online – hey, we all have our hobbies. But oh no, right after their nice little lie they just leave you there, barely giving you a second thought. Bastards.

And you'll get them at the boot sales too. The cut is not so deep as it is in the professional world. After all, you've already sacrificed your time at the Altar of the Boot, so frankly any conversation is a welcome distraction at this point.

As for money, well we've already covered that. So what have they left to take from you? Yep – your hopes.

These people will pick up nearly every item on your stall. They will ask you sensible and probing questions like, "What's this do?" and just when the glimmer hits your eyes that you may well be about to part with yet another Connect 4 – they put it down, and use their most evil incantation:

"I'll come back."

They won't. They. Will. Not. Come. Back. They'll pass you three or four more times and nod at you with the uncomfortable nod of someone caught in a lie. The truly evil ones may even fashion a smile at you, but one thing they will not do, that they will never do – is come back.

Some people are a little more interesting. I had a very nice little old lady – not an expression, she was old and she was little and she was a lady, ergo she was a little old lady – tell me that she didn't want to buy my espresso cups because she preferred to drink tea.

I told her I sympathised. I didn't buy a Kanye West* album because I prefer to listen to music.

Oh, and then there's the "You've got some nice stuff here," and then proceed to not buy any of it. Actually, that's really quite a nice thing to say to someone, so I'll let them have that.

In all fairness to these people, and so as to not come across as a total malcontent that has come off of his meds, I get it; these people are just being polite. However, what they fail to realise is that every time they rummage through a stall, they create just that little bit of hope in the mind of the seller. To have those hopes dashed only moments later will still smart, even if you've been doing these sales for years.

And isn't the truth so much more polite than some random platitude? What do these people think is going to happen if they just said, "Thanks very much. I'm not entirely sure I need this – really, I was more curious than anything. Perhaps if it's available later I may well reconsider. Until then, I bid you good day sir, and wish your attendance of this sale to prove to be a most fruitful endeavour."

Frankly if they did say that, I'm fairly sure I would give them the item for free and ask them if we could be friends on Facebook.

*Between starting this book and publishing it, Kanye West elected to change his name to Ye. I share this with you in order to stay current, but please, please, please do not mistake my doing this as an indication that I could care less.

Chapter 18 – Micro Trades

Some car boot exchanges are very brief. They don't deserve a chapter of their own but fall neatly into what I like to call Micro Trades. To be fair, as most of them don't actually result in a sale, the use of the word Trades could be construed as misleading. If that's an issue, please do take it up with your nearest solicitor – at the very least they'll give you a cup of tea whilst they listen to your case. Maybe even a biscuit. Then they'll throw you out.

Item – some plastic toy, I don't even know what it does.

The child asks how much it is and I reply, "50p." His father then starts barking at me from behind his kid. "20p."

No, I reply, it's 50p.

"30p." Classy – negotiating over 20p for a piece of plastic that you're going to give to your child as a gift, especially considering the child is holding said piece of plastic and witnessing the entire exchange. I just felt sorry for him, though not enough to sell it for less than 50p.

Item – Cable for a Walkman.

Guy was looking for a cable for a Walkman. I couldn't help but think that the only thing that you can plug into a Walkman are headphones and he had a pair on as he was speaking to me. Strange.

Item – Sky receiver.

Some people are weird about technology. My old Sky TV box is on display when the lady asks me if it works. I tell her it does. She asks if it's easy to plug in. I say that as long as she has a dish and the aerial plugs are visible then it should be easy. Then she asks the $64,000 question: "So if I plug this in, I'll get Sky for free?"

No madam. No you won't.

Item – Juicer

Man – "Working?"

Me – "Yes."

Man – "How much?"

Me – "Twenty-five pounds."

Man leaves. Perhaps if he considered having conversations rather than barking at people, I might have considered lowering my price. I mean I wouldn't, but he didn't know that, and just how much of a rush are you in at 7.15am on a Sunday in a field?

Item – A set of curtains, still in their packaging, brand new.

The lady asks me how much they are and I tell her they are £10. She inspects the packaging, asks about the size, how come I have brand-new curtains, etc. She then puts them down and is about to walk away when I say, "If ten pounds doesn't work for you then you're welcome to make me an offer."

"Oh it's not the price, it's the colour."

What? The colour you were aware of before ANY other piece of information. OK then.

Item – A flip chart displaying information which I thought could be of interest. Never actually for sale and if you read what's on the board, you can see that.

Man – "How much for this?"

Me – "You might want to take a closer look. In particular, the bit where it says – THIS FLIP CHART IS NOT FOR SALE."

Item – Not relevant.

Man – "How much?"

Me – "Make me an offer?"

Man – Grunts and walks away.

Me – "So even though I've told you that you can pay whatever you'd like, you still don't want it?"

Man – Repeats original grunt. Not sure what planet or indeed millennium he comes from, but I'm fairly sure they're not this one.

Chapter 19 – The Post-Purchase Millionaires

Like any good shop, your stall will be offering a spectrum of merchandise across a spectrum of prices. Anything from a 50p Peppa Pig plastic harmonica to a £25 juicer, you've got the lot.

Shoppers too, will be looking to spend across that spectrum. Some will have come out with a few quid in their pocket to simply take in the morning air and browse, whilst some will have got themselves cashed up and are on a mission to refurnish the entire ground floor of their house for less than the price of a year's subscription to Netflix. God bless them.

What you should know is that the majority of people coming up to your stand will fall somewhere neatly in between. They're aware that there are bargains to be had, but they would kick themselves if they had to pass up on the acquisition of a true bargain because they didn't bring enough money.

Now the more entrepreneurial amongst you may well invest in the means to take card payments on your phone, and if you're going into this as a business, then that's a good investment. Card payment machines will set you back around £50 and then you're looking at around 4.5% for every transaction. However, for the people parting with junk – save your money.

I'd also remind you that most buyers are also rummagers. They will happily turf everything you have over in the hopes of uncovering that one gem. Incidentally, if you have such items anywhere other than on prominent display, then I have taught you nothing and I hang my head in shame.

Enter the Post-Purchase Millionaire – more easily explained away with a tale.

PPM is happily rummaging through everything on the table. So far, she has uncovered two things which are of interest – The Peppa Pig plastic harmonica and a Minions fancy dress costume.

PPM – "How much for these two?"

Me – "Well the harmonica is 50p and the costume is two pound fifty, so that would be three pounds altogether."

PPM – "That's a lot." Is it? Is it really? Do you regularly buy fancy dress costumes for your children at under £2? If so, please tell me where you're shopping, because these World Book Days and birthday parties are really starting to break the bank.

PPM – "How about a pound for everything?"

Me – "I think even you know that's way too low, but I admire your conviction, so why don't we call it two?"

PPM – "How about one pound, fifty?"

Me – "Oh come on, the outfit on its own was supposed to go for two fifty, and you're asking me to give you that and the harmonica for less?"

PPM – "OK, two pounds."

At which point she reluctantly parts with her money, takes her items and goes. Oh that would have been nice wouldn't it? Except she doesn't go. She then proceeds to ask about all of the 'big ticket' items that I have on display.

This is a woman who just felt the need to negotiate to the tune of 50p who now, by some incredible turn of fate, is in a position to start shopping for the £20+ items that had been in front of her the whole time. And she's not just looking – oh no! She's asking questions, turning things over, giving them an examination that, under any other circumstances, would require the use of latex gloves and a certificate from at least three different medical boards.

And then she leaves. Of course she does! What else did I expect? That this 50p negotiation was in fact a test. The Grand Wizard has seen that I am indeed worthy of the quest to sell the juicer, for I have shown humility and great compassion, and she will now give me all of her money and lead me on the path to glory.

Yeah, not so much – she was just a pain in the arse.

Chapter 20 – The Mystery Item

This is not so much a lesson in negotiation as it is a plunder into the depths of the human psyche. A mystical journey that will leave you bewildered, astounded, and possibly a bit hungry, but in my defence, I have no way of knowing when you last ate.

And so, whatever the book equivalent of making the picture go all wobbly whilst someone plays a harp, I'm doing that now…gling gling gling…

The item in question was a USB cup warmer. Yes, I know – I'll explain. This was essentially a metal plate on a stand that you connected to your computer via one of its USB ports. When turned on, the metal plate would get hot and so if you kept your mug on there, your drink would stay warm.

The idea was originally put out amongst the promotional merchandise market, in hopes that this marvel of innovation would improve productivity, boost profits, and thereby send every small to medium-sized business into the stratosphere of financial glory.

In truth, it was less popular than the Microsoft Paper Clip (what, too soon?)

I had spent a number of years in the promotional merchandise industry (this is the part where I have to give a supposed 'shout out' to those from that industry that are now reading this book. Except this is not some pirate radio station broadcasting to the Yoof of Today, so stop it.)

As a result of being in this industry, over the years I had managed to rescue a number of unwanted product samples from going in the bin. I would regularly take said items to a boot sale, and would donate any proceeds from the sale of those items to my company's chosen charity – see? What a nice man I am.

And so, with no box, manual or care in the world, the USB cup warmer found its way onto my table one sunny, Sunday morning in a field.

And the next Sunday, and the one after that, and the year after that too. I literally could not give this thing away. What was interesting however, is just how many people picked it up in the time that it was there. More interesting than that, is the order in which the questions came. Now, see if you can keep up here, because this does tend to get a little complicated.

Question 1 – How much is this please?

Question 2 – And what is it?

As the brakes of your brain bring your thinking process to a shrieking halt, let's take a look at that again, except this time, let's put the questions in the order usually adopted by people with enough functioning brain cells to remain upright:

Question 1 – What is this please?

Question 2 – And how much is it?

Do you see how much more sense that makes? People actually wanted to know the price of something, before they wanted to assess if it was something they even needed at all! This went on for so long that my answer to Question 1 changed, which made the conversation so much more fun:

Question 1 – How much is this please?

Answer – I'll tell you what my friend. That particular item has travelled this great country, and indeed this planet in hopes of finding a home that would show it some love and attention. If you can tell me what it is, I'll let you have it for free.

The warmer stayed with me over two seasons of car boot sales, until someone actually came up and asked, "How much for the cup warmer?" and I hugged him as we agreed upon the price.

Chapter 21 – High Street Fashion at Knock Down Prices

Whilst many people's claims of brand new could hold about as much water as a Poundland paddling pool with a hole in it, when you're standing in a field trying to part with your junk, you'll be sharing that space with professional traders who are selling genuinely brand-new merchandise.

There are a number of reasons why brand-new items end up with these traders. They could have bought from companies going into liquidation. It could be a warehouse suffering from either flood or fire damage, whereby the items can no longer be sold through traditional retail channels. If you're talking about jewellery, some stores are required to return display pieces after they've been tried out by a certain number of people, as they're no longer considered 'brand new'.

That last one worked particularly well for me at one point. I purchased a watch that retailed for £400. I paid £69. I wore it for a couple of years and then sold it online for £200. Not at a boot sale, so no lesson here – I'm just pretty pleased with myself, so ner!

Other traders simply have great relationships with warehouses and are able to buy at very low prices, mark up accordingly, and essentially pass that saving on to you. Every once in a while, it pays to go to a boot sale as a buyer, just to see what you might pick up.

The trouble is that there will be some 'customers' who are literally too stupid to tell the difference between a legitimate market trader and a bloke trying to sell off the junk from his garage.

This was sadly brought home to me by a young lady who will be given the buyer code FFS. It stands for exactly what you think it stands for, as this really was the only reaction I could muster.

FFS – "This is jumper?" Yep – set the tone early. Pick up a knitted garment with two sleeves, a hole for the head to go through, establish that it's too short to be a dress and then ask if it's a jumper.

Me – "No – that's actually the International Space Station. They said they'd pretty much learned all they had to up there so they asked if I could find a home for it." I didn't say any of these words. My response was more along the lines of "Yes, it's a jumper."

FFS – "Is for boy?"

Me – "Well it was my son's, but I see no reason why a girl couldn't wear it if she wanted to."

FFS – "What age is for?"

Me – (It's four, isn't it?) "I think it says it on the label there – probably age 7-8."

FFS – "How much you want?"

Me – "All the clothes on the rail are one pound."

FFS – "Will you take 50p because it's a bit…" trails off in the hopes that I will fill in the blanks, but oh no – you started it madam, so you can finish it.

Me – "A bit what?"

FFS – "Used."

Me – "Do you know where you are right now? Do you need me to call someone?" Again, I just couldn't say it out loud – "Well they're all used. That's why I'm asking for one pound."

Now it turns out that whilst she was using the word 'used', what she actually meant was 'bobbly'. Yes, like any woollen garment, some bobbles had formed on the surface, but in my defence IT'S A BLOODY BOOT SALE AND I'M ASKING FOR A SOLITARY POUND!!!!!!!

FFS – "Yes but, you can see…" and then proceeds to point out each and every bobble, blissfully unaware that I got the point after the first twelve of them.

Now it's worth pointing out that this exchange took place in what was scheduled to be the last of my car boot adventures for the year. Any item of clothing which did not sell today would not be coming back for another try. They would be loaded into bin bags and dropped off at the nearest charity shop. The bags were already in the car – I was coming home with an empty boot, one way or the other.

Me – "OK, you can have it for 50p."

She used the 50p that she saved to buy a Ming vase. The owner wanted £6.5 million for it, but she argued him down because it was, in her own words, "a bit old".

Chapter 22 – The Generation Gap

I am a self-confessed lover of all things gadget. As a voice over artist, the majority of my nerdgasms are over all things audio. From microphones to mixing desks to digital processors that can make you sound like a Dalek, every so often I will treat myself. I'm still looking for the gadget that can make me sound like an original Cylon from *Battlestar Galactica*, but some treasures are left in the begotten analogue age.

After that are all the little digital video and stills cameras for capturing every magical moment – from filming my opening the box on my brand-new toy to filming my putting it back in the box in order to sell. Always keep your boxes by the way – they seriously add value.

And naturally, like all gadgets, eventually these shiny boxes with blinky lights get replaced by shinier boxes with blinkier lights. And so it will go on...forever and ever...until I die. And probably afterwards too, unless my death just happens to coincide with the end of civilisation as we know it, which I would like to think is unlikely.

Many of the gadgets will find themselves on eBay or similar sites and will fetch decent money. On the other hand, though, is the stuff that surfs the razor's edge between 'bit too cool for car boot' and 'bit too crap for eBay'.

My advice? And it would seem odd, if at this stage of reading, you didn't want it – is to do both. At the time of writing, research carried out by *The Gadget Show* indicates that the best time to list something on eBay is on a Sunday at around 6.30pm, taking around 64% of the traffic of the week. After that, it's Monday at around 8pm, but only for 11%.

The good news is that your boot sale is going to be on either a Saturday or Sunday. So, post your item, have a reserve price in mind, and then take it to your sale and ask for the same figures.

Thereafter, you can politely decline any silly offers by telling buyers that it is currently listed on eBay and that you're happy to wait to see how that pans out. Have the listing on your phone ready to show people and tell them they have the advantage of not having to a) pay for delivery and b) wait for delivery. Strangely enough, your more serious purchaser will actually start coming around.

Gadgets are indeed a great draw, and therefore if you have a box, prop the items up on it. Try and create some levels on your table and put the best stuff up high. Small and fiddly goes at the front and make sure that if any cables are required, that they're tucked away neatly and tied up with a cable tie.

Of course, none of that actually matters because within about thirty minutes your table will be a state and you'll have tired of constantly moving things into a nice position only for the next customer to move them straight back out again.

Invariably, you are going to find yourself face to face with someone who is, for the best part, window shopping.

Look, this would probably be so much easier to explain in a tale – obviously – it's kind of the whole point.

Customer here shall be given the code CNB – Clearly Not Buying.

CNB – "What this?" It would be non-PC of me to point out that the gentleman was not born upon these shores. Or within the last hundred years. So I won't be doing that.

Me – "It's a business card scanner."

CNB – "What for?"

Me – "Well you connect it to your computer, and when someone gives you their card, you scan it and then you don't need to clutter up your office with cards."

CNB – "Oh...what this?"

Me – "That is a SCART lead."

CNB – "OK, OK, SCART lead. And this one?"

Me – "That's a FireWire cable."

CNB – "It's for computer?"

And this is when you realise that you have a moral obligation to get rid of this person. There's a simple rule when it comes to buying computer accessories at a boot sale – if you have to ask what it is, then it has absolutely no place in your life. I need to politely tell this man to put his money away, although to be fair, at this stage he hasn't actually taken out any money.

Me – "If I may be very straight with you here, that's a fairly specialist piece of equipment. If you have to ask me what it is, I get the sense that you probably have no need for it, and I would not want to waste your time."

We all know that the subtext here is that I don't want him wasting my time, but at least in that version I came across as a considerate and compassionate man, simply unwilling to take the money of the weak and vulnerable. They should make me a saint – I should get a national holiday!

Nah – the bloke was just annoying me, and I really needed a wee.

Chapter 23 – The Not-So-Shrewd Negotiator

Some people are born negotiators. When they're working their magic, it's a genuine privilege to just sit back and watch a master at work. Every gesture, every word and every well-constructed pause is all woven together to produce a dialogue between buyer and seller that transcends the mere exchange of goods for money and approaches what can be best described as a religious experience.

Most people however, are just crap at it. Unfortunately, they believe that they are the car boot equivalent of the Wolf of Wall Street and will waste no time in getting straight down to business. However, if you, as the owner of the goods, does not do everything in your power to have fun with these people, then I fear that I have taught you nothing, and I'll have to get you to start waxing my car and painting my fence again.

These 'buyers', and I air quote for reasons which will become apparent, are merely there to play. Their acquisition of your goods comes second to their screwing you down to the lowest possible price, blissfully unaware that, all the while, you are literally asking them to give you money to take away your junk.

Keep that in mind and you will always, ALWAYS have the upper hand. Factor in that you're being asked to negotiate over about 50p, and it becomes all too obvious just why it is your right, nay, your God-given duty, to enjoy every minute of the negotiation. You literally have nothing to lose.

To illustrate my point, we shall first attempt to sell two bicycle helmets. The buyer here will be ascribed the code RAM – Rather Aggressive Mother:

RAM – "How much is the helmet?"

Me – "It's three pounds for that."

RAM – "THREE???????" Now yes, the word coming out of her mouth was "three" but the tone was more akin to "You come into my farm in the middle of night, eat three live chickens and then do unspeakable things to my goat?????"

I felt a sense of shame. How could I, a mild-mannered man of too little hair and too high a body mass index do such a thing? To ask such an unreasonable amount for these mere trinkets, and in front of her children. I carefully pondered my reply.

Me – "No, you're right, that's far too cheap. Let's say five."

RAM then spends the next few minutes inspecting these helmets in great detail. Well, I say great detail – she did put a Hello Kitty helmet meant for a four-year-old girl on her seven-year-old son but hey, I'm not judging. Who am I kidding? This whole book is based on the fundamental principle of my judging.

RAM – "Would you take one-fifty?"

Me – "I'm sorry, no. I think three pounds is a fair price. Why don't we agree upon two pounds?"

RAM – "If I take both helmets, would you do them for three fifty?" Do you see what's happening here? The price is no longer relevant. What this woman wants is a win – a chance to put one over on the poor, unsuspecting stall holder who, at this point has already mentally checked out of the entire conversation and is going over a recipe for sous vide duck breast in his mind.

Me – "No, I'll do them for four pounds because you've already got me down from six."

RAM – "Yes but they don't really need them you see." RAM points out the two boys that are with her.

At this point I fail to understand her logic. Actually, that's not really accurate – I am acutely aware of the fact that logic left this conversation before it even started. Surely if you don't really need something then its actual value to you is zero. Why not just walk away? I promise I won't think any less of you, but then given the bar you've set at this point, I really wouldn't have anywhere left to go.

OK, I can see we're going to have to take the long way round on this one.

Me – "I understand. Well if they don't really need them then they'll be twenty pounds."

RAM – "What? That's way too expensive. And as I said, they don't really need
them, so I'm not paying twenty pounds for them."

Me – "Indeed. But at this stage you've also told me that you're not paying four pounds for them either. If, as you say, they don't need them, then paying sixteen pounds more than you want to is technically the same as paying fifty pence more, wouldn't you agree?"

RAM reaches into her purse for the £4 and buys the helmets, and I thank the gods that the ordeal is coming to a close. But OH NO! The fun does not stop there. She then spots an armband, suitable for runners to insert their mobile phones. I bought it a couple of years ago, tried it, didn't like it and shoved it in a drawer, so here it was.

RAM – "How much for the armband?"

Me – "It's a pound for that. Retailed at twelve and I only used it once, so it really is as good as new."

RAM – "Would you take 50p for it?"

Me – "No."

RAM – "Even though we've already bought a lot of stuff from you today?" I should stress that there is not even a shred of irony in this woman's voice.

Me – "Well, to be fair, you've bought two bicycle helmets, and whilst I'm grateful for your business, I doubt there are many people that would refer to two items as 'a lot'. Secondly, I actually want two pounds for the armband but as I knew you would attempt to halve any figure I presented to you, I just decided to save each other both some time and tell you the price I figured you'd eventually argue me down to."

RAM – "Well I've leave it and I'll come back later and if it's still here then maybe you'll let me have it for 50p."

Me – "If it is, then absolutely."

I counted the hours, desperate to catch just one last glimpse of this vision of grace and diplomacy. Not really – I went and bought an ice cream. But just to wrap this story up with a nice little bow, RAM did return about two hours later.

RAM – "Is that armband still here?"

Me – "I'm afraid not, it went about three minutes after you left and for the price I wanted."

RAM walked away, defeated, but none the less ready to inflict her own form of torture on some other unsuspecting stall holder on another day. I, on the other hand, was left to wonder what sort of parent gambles with their children's safety over a matter of 50p.

Chapter 24 – The Powerful Carrier Bag

In the world of professional sales, cross-selling and upselling are par for the course. As consumers, we're exposed to it every day, from the "Do you want fries with that?" to the extended warranty on your new dishwasher, we are always being upsold.

At a car boot sale, that option really isn't there. It would just be weird to ask your customer if he or she would like a pair of binoculars to go with their new Connect 4.

However, one should never rule it out. On one occasion a lady purchased a pair of children's trainers from me. I wanted £2 but she only wanted to pay £1 and it was getting late in the day, so I agreed.

She then asked me if I had a carrier bag and the only one I could find that was actually rather nice and I just didn't want to give it to someone buying just one item for half its allocated value. So I dug a little deeper and found a massive bag that was just way too big for a tiny pair of shoes.

Lady – "That's a big bag."

Me – "I'm sorry, but it's all I've got left. Tell you what though, why don't you buy a few more things and then the bag will make a lot more sense!"

AND SHE DOES!

Now I'm not saying a trick like that is going to work every time, but seriously – what have you got to lose?

Chapter 25 – The Marvellous Machine

Now, as a writer, I have to be very careful when speaking about overcoming language barriers. Do it right, and the comedy ensues and we all enjoy a jolly good tickling of the ribs. Do it wrong, and certain people will brandish this book as part of some hate-fuelled racist manifesto and order that every copy be burned immediately and that I be hunted down as an enemy of the people.

There are two things wrong with that. First – at the time of writing, this book has only been planned to be published electronically, so that is going to prove to be one very expensive bonfire, and second – can we all just calm down a bit please? I live in a multicultural city in a multicultural country. I myself am the son of an Egyptian refugee and only a very small percentage of my family are English and living here.

That said, if someone's poor grasp of the English language causes me to either smile, laugh or just flat out take the piss, then it would simply be bad for my internal organs to hold in such rhetoric.

Customer in question shall be called 3M, which stands for Marvellous Magical Machine. Over the years I have acquired a lot of cables. USB, SCART, FireWire, telephone, the blue one that goes into the thing – you know…the thing? Anyway, lots of cables. They're essentially useless to me now as the machines to which they belonged either died or got sold, and altogether I've been able to put together three plastic containers filled with cables.

Now good news for me is that I actually know what I have in there. If you come up and ask me for an HDMI cable, I can instantly tell you that I don't have one. However, if you'd like an RS232 cable for a printer that you kept from 1986, then Bob's your uncle. Sure, you may laugh, but there are plenty of hobbyists out there that collect old tech, and if you have the rare means to help them get that tech working, then you are sitting on a veritable gold mine.

Up comes 3M and proceeds to pick up and examine every single cable. No, sorry, that sentence needed a bit more punctuation – every…single…cable.

After what felt like an eternity I decided to see if I could accelerate this man's desperate treasure hunt:

Me – "Is there a specific cable you're after? I can save you some time there."

3M – "I look for cable." And so the dance begins.

Me – "Yes, I can see that. Was there a certain cable you needed?"

3M – "I look for cable."

Me – "Right. Well that's you just saying the same thing as before isn't it? What cable are you looking for?"

Now surely you've realised that at this point, I have accepted that I can play a delicate balance of good customer service and sarcastic wit. It's really more of a coping mechanism for me, because as it turns out, people get rather upset when you just start randomly throwing heavy objects in their general direction.

3M – "Is for machine."

Me – "It's for a machine?"

3M – "Yes, is for machine."

Me – "OK well I'm no engineer but I think even Isambard Kingdom Brunel might need a little more to go on. What machine is it for?"

3M – "Is for machine."

Me – "Well I suppose all of these are for a machine, but I don't think you want to buy all of my cables. What does the machine do?"

3M – "Is machine. Is shaver."

Me – "Oh, it's for a shaver? Electric shaver?" Yes all right smart arse, I realise you don't have to plug in a traditional razor but at this point I really had lost the will to live. "No I'm sorry, I don't have that."

3M – "Oh OK. Thank you."

And you'd think that would be the end of it. Except you would be wrong. 3M then proceeds to spend another five full minutes examining the remaining cables before finally walking away.

I could have asked him if there was anything else he needed, but I'd actually just sold my last slap across the head with a rubber chicken, so there wasn't really anything more I could do for him.

Chapter 26 – And Your Point Is????

Someone once said, "Always be the smartest person in the room." That's good advice, but if you go around acting like you believe it, then most people will dismiss you as a dickhead, long before they respect your intelligence.

Sometimes though, you'll find yourself in an exchange that leaves you confident that you are not only the smartest person in the room, or in this case, field - but that you are, in all fairness, on the short end of an exchange with a complete and total muppet.

Under those circumstances, there really is only one thing left to do. Let the games begin…

The item in question was a charger. I don't remember now what it charged but it was brand new, never used and I had done my research. I knew that a new one in the shops was £20. Now we both know that the retail value is about as relevant as a corned beef and pickle sandwich at this point, but I figure you've earned the right to some context. After all, you've come this far.

Actually, I'm quite in the mood for a corned beef and pickle sandwich now, which is unfortunate on a number of levels – the primary one being my abundant lack of corned beef. Or pickle. Or bread. Christ, I really do need to do some shopping.

The muppet in question shall be referred to as YTW – Young Tracksuit Wearer. His accent, and indeed the tracksuit, which seems to be some sort of uniform for his demographic, suggested that he was from somewhere in Eastern Europe, but I really could not narrow it down and doing so does very little for the narrative anyway.

YTW – "This charger?" The item in question has a three-pronged UK plug on one end, and a cable coming out of it with a micro USB cable on the other, so in all fairness, WHAT THE BLOODY HELL ELSE COULD IT BE???

Me – "Yes. It's micro USB so really any Android phone and of course a lot of other devices too."

YTW – "How much you want?"

Me – "It's five pounds. Good price because they're twenty pounds new." Yeah, I know, but he was making that face. You know – that face?

YTW – "Well I'm buying it for somebody else so..." He makes alternative face to ask for a lower price without saying the actual words.

It's an odd negotiating tactic isn't it? One has to wonder how they think it's going to play out. Start a sentence with the suggestion that you would like to pay less, then tail off before you actually finish. Surely at that point I would not only let him have the item for free but would also let him drive it away in my car because, gosh darned it to heck, he's just so darn clever!

Me – "I'm not really sure that's relevant. The price is five pounds."

YTW – "Will you take two pounds because I don't even know if it works."

Me – And by this point I had both barrels loaded – "So, just to understand your position, you're prepared to pay less for the item in case it doesn't work but by the same logic, you're more than happy to pay for broken merchandise. Not only that, but you'd also be content to gift that broken merchandise to somebody else?"

AHAAAAAA! Hoisted with your own petard sir! Feel the cut of my steely logic and rapier wit! To quote Lord Vader himself, "You are beaten. It is useless to resist."

These internal monologues of personal victory are all that's left to keep me sane, so please just let me have them. Or the corned beef sandwich – really, either is fine.

YTW left with no charger. Now I get it – when you're buying electronic merchandise you are taking a risk, and this person decided that he was more comfortable risking £2 than he was risking £5. But here's the thing – if he wanted to completely remove that risk from the equation, he could have gone to a shop and paid £20. He would have received a warranty, and maybe even a nice little bag to put it in, although chances are he would have preferred to save himself the extra 5p.

His problem was that all of his arguments were not logical. So what if we was buying it for someone else? As far as I'm concerned, once you've bought it from me you really can do whatever you like with it – give it to a friend, share it with a colleague, chuck it in the frickin' river – I don't care, and I'm sure as hell not going to more than halve my prices just because you don't want to keep it for yourself.

As it was, the charger sold later that morning for the original asking price of £5. I used the money to buy a sandwich – no prizes for guessing which, and I understand that the buyer used the charger to overthrow a dictatorship in South America. Like I say, once it's out of my hands…

Chapter 27 – Your Hands Probably Work – A Side Note

Whilst this is something that I've noticed at car boot sales, this really is just a gripe that I'd like to get off my chest.

What's with all these people walking around boot sales with Bluetooth earpieces hanging out one side of their face?

I mean seriously, how many calls are you realistically taking at 6.30am on a Sunday morning? And even if someone is calling you, what's wrong with actually reaching into your pocket, taking out your phone and putting it to your frickin' ear?

Sure, I understand – there are people that think that using an earpiece protects them from the dangerous radiation being emitted by their phone – the very same phone currently residing in a pocket next to either their heart or their genitals, both of which are soaking up all that lovely irradiating goodness that comes from a halfway decent Bluetooth signal.

And even if you are protecting your health, you still look like an arsehole. What image are you trying to share with us? That you're some captain of industry that knows that amongst all of this second-hand junk is the Ming vase or Van Gogh that would look just stunning in your corporate office – by which I mean your downstairs toilet?

"Hi darling. Yeah, it looks like a genuine da Vinci. It's probably worth around fifteen million but I reckon I can get the guy down to three pounds. Shall I go for it?"

Get real sunshine and get that thing out of your ear. Besides, everyone knows you'll never get a da Vinci for less than a tenner.

Chapter 28 – The £1.74 Paradox

Lack of sufficient funds is rarely, if ever, an effective bargaining strategy. Strange as it may seem though, there are still some people that believe that they can walk into a Ferrari showroom, tell the salespeople that they only have enough for the bus ride home, and yet still drive out in their brand-new sports car.

These people are - and I'll choose my words carefully here – morons. Here I am, standing out in a field somewhere in the unwelcoming early hours of a Sunday morning. I spent hours putting my stuff together, broke a sweat loading the car up at 'Bloody Early' o'clock and then compounded that sweat at the other end unloading the car and setting everything up, all at a time when the only people awake are farmers, night-shift workers and hard-core clubbers currently off their faces on a heady combination of alcopops and doner kebabs. I'm tired, and despite being excited about the possibility of enjoying a fun-filled morning of delightful banter, am seriously not in the mood to put up with people pleading poverty.

And this delightful rant leads me to the star of our next exchange. In my most recent car boot sale, my wife and I had painstakingly gone through all of our children's cupboards to clear out any clothes which no longer fitted them.

Socks, underwear and anything which could only really be thought of as a rag for washing the car, were instantly taken to the array of clothing banks at our local recycling centre. If you don't live near to a recycling centre, you can still find these banks in the car parks of major supermarkets, or sometimes outside of civil buildings like police stations, fire stations and libraries. Failing that, a quick online search will tell you where your nearest recycling centre is, so I'm sure you'll find one.

All the remaining items were divided up into large plastic storage boxes according to gender and age. They don't need to go in neatly, because they will be in a state within three minutes of people going anywhere near them, and that's totally fine.

The mentality of selling clothes at a boot sale, especially children's clothes, is simple – whatever doesn't sell is going to a charity shop. Now this is an important point, and it comes back to the primary reason we are there – to get rid of stuff. Remember the Car Boot Mantra:

These people are paying me to clean my house.

What this means is that you simply cannot be precious about any item there when it comes to price. If you have got some really nice pieces that you think would fetch 'proper' money, then post them on eBay, Gumtree or Facebook Marketplace – I imagine I'm legally obliged (turns out I'm not, but I've started this now) to point out that other auction and car boot websites are available, but do you seriously think I'm going to waste both mine and your time listing them all? Chances are another five would have launched in the time it took me to write this sentence, although I will give a mention to Shpock which I think is pretty good.

Now when it comes to selling clothes, it's a good idea to get hold of a rail. This becomes a delicate balancing act. You see a good and sturdy clothing rail, as used by professional market traders, will set you back something in the region of £30, which means you need to have a lot of clothes to put on there to make it worthwhile.

Conversely, you can pick up substantially cheaper clothes rails but you're then going to find yourself picking up all of your clothes from the ground every half hour or so, as the slightest gust of wind will turn all of your precious garments into one giant windsock.

As for children's clothes, those can just be placed into plastic storage boxes or even cardboard boxes if that's all you have available. Some people just lay down a massive plastic sheet and spread the clothes all around for people to rummage through. Personally, I think that looks scrappy, but if clothes are your leading item, it can be a good way to go. Of course, you need to keep a closer watch on your stuff as, regrettably some customers will have very sticky fingers. No not thieves, I'm talking kids and ice cream – they make a right mess.

So, let's take a look at pricing. Trying to assign prices to each individual item will melt your brain faster than an episode of *Love Island*, so make life easier on yourself. I worked to a very simple scheme – coats and jackets were £2, dresses were £1 and everything else was 50p. Also, if they buy a whole bunch of stuff, there'll probably be a discount on there for them too.

So, we have the context, and our players are in position, so let us enter the narrative. The role of 'Moron' will be given the code MFS, which stands for Middle-aged, Foreign and Slow, although by the end of this, I'm fairly sure you'll think it stands for something else:

MFS – "How much you want these T-shirt? Is for charity." Granted, I cannot say from which foreign shore our visitor hailed, and I certainly didn't care enough to ask.

Me – "Well you have two shirts there and they're 50p each, so that will be one pound please."

MFS .... These dots are to indicate the passing of time between my giving him the most basic of explanations and his formulating a response.

MFS – "One pound it is?"

Me – "That's right, one pound. If you'd like to buy more clothes, then I'll happily give you a discount."

MFS – "Oh." (skip the dots, just assume they're there. Seriously, I could have made these shirts by the time he responded).

He then reaches into his pocket and proceeds to pull out 74p.

MFS – "This is all I have on me." And then starts chuckling in a weird way which is half uncomfortable and has me half considering the very real possibility that this man is having a stroke.

Me – "Really?" You have to understand that the majority of people who claim that the amount that they have just pulled out of their pockets is 'all they have on them' are, for the most part, lying sods. It would be lovely to live in a world where my default position was to trust everyone, but sadly, this just isn't so.

MFS – continues to chuckle. OK, not a stroke but now definitely uncomfortable.

Now before you start saying "Awwww" and think I'm some unfeeling rogue trader who wouldn't look out of place in Mos Eisley space port (if that means nothing to you, I simply cannot help you), let me tell you that I did, in fact, let him have the shirts for the 74p. Am I really going to argue with this person over 26p? The sheer time it would take for him to understand the concept is more than any sane person should ever have to endure.

Me – "OK then my friend, you have yourself a deal." Strange to think that the saving of 26p could be considered a 'deal' in anyone's vocabulary, but this guy is clearly in need of a win, so I let him have it.

I took his money. It's what happened next which really annoyed me. MFS then proceeded to look through all of the other clothing boxes on my stand!

What is this moron doing??? He has just openly stated that he has now spent his last remaining 74p on my two T-shirts and yet now he wants to make a mess of my stand and for what? Window shopping?

And what's the deal with telling me that it's for charity? Granted, he doesn't know this, but the fact is that everything that doesn't sell here is going to charity anyway. I don't need some 'handler' to take care of the more subtle nuances of dropping off a sack of clothes at the Cancer Research shop – it really is a remarkably simple process. If you're not sure, let me talk you through it:

Step 1 – Put unwanted clothes in bin liner
Step 2 – Take bin liner to charity shop
Step 3 – Leave charity shop

There you go – not only are you being entertained here, but you're getting valuable life hacks too. Incidentally, when did a 'handy tip' become a 'life hack'? True hacking involves a process of breaking through a multitude of security procedures in order to access and manipulate data to which said hacker would previously not have had permission to do so. Teaching someone how to best take a stone out of an avocado is not hacking.

Hold on a second, I've realised that I'm now enjoying a rant within a rant – an uber rant, if you will. Kind of like *Inception*, but with a premise that my wife can actually understand. Let's go back to the first rant...

And another thing whilst my blood is boiled to the sufficient level to melt steel: my stand was near the entrance – I got there early enough to ensure that. Therefore, given that I saw that this gentleman was carrying no other purchases, and taking into account the fact that he would have paid

£1 to get in, I am led to ask one very simple question. Who the F£$%&^!!! comes to a car boot sale with only £1.74??

This guy just clearly has not thought things through. You don't blow over half the money in your pocket on the price of admission. That's like going to Disneyland and only leaving yourself $1 for the assortment of unnecessary crap that your kids will continually beg you to buy until you either submit or lay down on the tracks of the nearest rollercoaster and await the sweet release of death.

Listen, I get it – some people are just poor planners. My wife has been quick to point out that it is slightly unfair of me to judge anyone without full knowledge of their backstory and she is 100% right. However, I have had to point out that the snap judgements I make of people are, in fact, the very building blocks of this book, and if I started to come across as all cuddly and sympathetic, then the persona of 'impatient and judgmental bastard' that I have so carefully crafted will get ever so slightly dissolved.

So sure, some people make look upon this man with pity. Perhaps even a sense of melancholy, blended beautifully with an epic tale of lost love, worldly adventures and heroic deeds of epic proportions.

I, however, formed a shortlist and you're welcome to tick the appropriate box:

1. He was a moron
2. He was a lying git

Chapter 29 – The Wild Card

It's often occurred to me that my entire car boot selling experience could be made so much more fun by having my brain chemistry altered by alcohol.

Sadly, there are several things which serve as a barrier to such endeavours. The first is that having a car boot is intrinsically linked with having a car, and said car being driven – by me. You'll remember I said that you needed an understanding partner to do this? Well that doesn't extend to asking them if they could drive you to a field at 5am because you're off your face – you really can only push a relationship so far.

Of course, the more entrepreneurial drinkers amongst you may well be thinking that I could show up sober, set up my stand and then down a couple of cheeky Jäegerbombs to really throw a match on this metaphorical bucket of petrol.

Well no. There are several things wrong with that plan. First – once I've finished, I still have to drive home ("Darrrlllliinnnngg – I love you, you're my besht friend. Can you come and get me?" Not going to happen).

Second, whilst the nearest burger van will avail me of the greasy treats to aid me on my journey back to sobriety, that journey involves a stopover in obesity, with delightful views of energy loss and heart failure, so I'd prefer to give it a miss.

And third – and I fear that, in all this excitement that you may well have missed this point – it's six o'clock in the bloody morning! I need a good hour of standing up in a cold field before I can even contemplate my first Red Bull. Seriously – who are you people?

Being drunk at a car boot sale is not an option for a seller. However, for a buyer, the same is not true, and despite the social faux pas of being off one's face at 8.30 on a Sunday morning, at least one drunken twat will skip church to come and worship at the altar that is all things boot.

Now I'm not one to stereotype. No, wait – actually I am. I really, really am – it's only the threat of this book being pulled off the shelves by the PC brigade that keeps my stereotyping in check.

Suffice to say that whatever image you have of the drunken person that's made his or her (usually his) way to your stand of an early weekend morning, you are pretty much spot on.

If all of the regular tell-tale signs allude you, then just listen out for the little voice in your head saying, "Go away, go away, go away, go away, go away, oh shit he's coming over," and you'll soon get the idea.

Now regaling you of any specific tale of a half drunken exchange – two people, one of us is drunk, the other is not – would be tricky. Sadly, they are just not all that memorable. On my part there's just nothing interesting said and on their part, their brain hasn't formed a memory for a good twenty years.

The good news is that they all follow the same pattern, hence here is every car boot drunken exchange in one go.

The customer shall be given the code PGA – Please Go Away.

PGA – "Ag fleben…ddis you wiv a hahahahaha!"

Me – "Indeed."

PGA – "Ha ma da?"

Me – "Twenty quid."

PGA – "Ya wah?"

Me – "Thirty quid." Please understand that the quoted price here is irrelevant – this person will not, and indeed, cannot buy anything. Their lack of funds is only eclipsed by their lack of functioning brain cells, and the ever-present threat of impending violence means I may as well have a laugh.

PGA – "Ohhhhh ha ha ha ha – is a firty is eh??"

Me – "Well I hear there's a bloke over there doing them for cheaper."

PGA – "Ah ma. Weh dee. OK."

And so PGA walks away, armed with nothing more than half a can of Special Brew, a wild sense of ambition, and a Tesco carrier bag with a hole in it. The local headmaster really does let himself go on the weekends.

Chapter 30 – The Rummagers

When I was about 16 years old, I got a Saturday job at Currys, the electrical retail store. In those days, the shops were on the high street, rather than on an industrial park, and it was possible to walk around the entire store within fifteen minutes, thus negating the modern need of several hours, a Sherpa to guide you, and a light snack when you've made it to the headphone section and are not sure you have enough energy to make it all the way to the fridges at the back.

The good news is that some things have not changed – you still have a one in fifty chance of finding a member of staff who actually knows anything about the products on display. Sure, some of them will bluff their way through by reading the little ticket next to the price, but spending too much time with said individuals will result in one of only two outcomes:

You will hurt these people physically, or
Your brain will fall out of your arse.

That is, of course, if you can actually find a member of staff to help you in the first place. Remember, some of them set off from the staff room at 9am, and it's a 16-mile hike to the microwaves.

Anyway, back to my point. In addition to selling stuff (which – and this may surprise you – I was quite good at), one of the other things I loved doing was merchandising.

This was particularly true at Christmas, where we would strip out the window displays and create something new and enticing. Careful planning and consideration would go into the placement of each item, taking the would-be customer on a journey which we hoped would end with their entering our store and making a purchase.

Such merchandising, or 'window dressing' skills would serve me well throughout my career, from setting up showrooms in my promotional merchandise company, to the creation of stands at exhibitions and conferences. It's an important skill and one I'm proud to have honed throughout the years.

And at a car boot sale, it's close to completely pointless.

Once you've parked in your allocated space, all thoughts of merchandising will quickly give way to just getting the stuff out of the car as quickly as possible, at which point you will realise that there is no way on Earth that everything you've brought is going to fit on the table, hence we enter the realm of creative stacking.

Creative stacking is the art of grouping a bunch of items together which all loosely fall under the same category, and then placing the largest one on the bottom and building a small tower. Take board games, for example – if someone takes a look at your KerPlunk, then there's a good chance that they might be interested in the Battleships nestled underneath that. And if they've gone that far, perhaps they might dare to venture forth onto level 3 – the Monopoly set which both enhanced and simultaneously destroyed so many family Christmases.

And so you build. And then you look at the half full box of stuff still on the back seat. So, you redesign, and you build again, and possibly even again, because God forbid that early buyer was looking for the deck of playing cards that you hadn't set out yet! I mean that's a clear 20p down the drain right there – you IDIOT!

Sadly however, all of your efforts will mostly be in vain, and the reason is because the vast majority of buyers at boot sales are rummagers.

These people fully accept that there is no real system in place whatsoever on your stand. You're like a miniature Woolworths – you sell lots of stuff, but if anybody asked you what you actually sell, you wouldn't be able to tell them.

As such, your early morning display which you believe could surely rival Selfridges windows at Christmas, is really only going to serve to entice a small percentage of the buying population. The rest of them will think nothing of rummaging through your boxes before you've even finished taking the stuff out, so don't worry about it.

By all means, do put your best foot forward, placing high value items in prominent positions on your table, and make a point of keeping things neat so that people can have a good look around. However, if your table is getting crowded, just leave your boxes out for people to go through. Trust me, if you have what they're looking for – bearing in mind that they have no idea what that actually is – then they will find it.

Other rummagers are just plain weird. You will encounter the occasional buyer that will pick up everything on your stand and not buy anything, but just recently I had an encounter with a rummager which stuck in my memory.

Over the years I have amassed an insane number of cables. Audio cables, SCART leads, FireWire, USB – I've got loads and I use very few of them. Looking on eBay, I saw that these were not totally worthless, with people paying up to £3 for a USB cable. So I sorted them out into categories, put them into some plastic shoeboxes, and put them on display.

A more dedicated, and perhaps thoughtful stall holder may well have taken the time to put a cable tie around each of them to avoid everything getting tangled, but I am not, so I did not. And they did.

By the third sale, these boxes contained lovely piles of cable spaghetti, and I simply could not be bothered to do anything about it. The most popular cables were being sold for a pound and the more specialist stuff went for between £3 and £5, so with those sorts of bargains in mind, I figured I would let the buyers sort through the mess.

Enter the customer, who shall be given the code RRR, which stands for Rummage, Rummage, Rummage. I can't tell you any more about her because she never spoke, but her actions warranted her inclusion in this book.

Now bear in mind that there are not one, not two, but three boxes of cable spaghetti to wade through. RRR heads to box one and picks up a cable. She examines the end of it and sees the USB connection on one end. She then carefully trails the cable through her fingers, finds the other end, sees the mini USB connection and puts it down.

Fair enough, I think – mini USB is becoming more and more obsolete, which would probably explain why I have a whole frickin' box of them.

RRR then proceeds to pick up another cable and do the exact same thing. She checks out the connection at one end, carefully disentangles the cable, sees it's exactly the same as her previous effort, and puts it back.

This happens again, and again, and again, until she has carefully examined three USB leads, 2 FireWire cables, one RF lead, a couple of SCART connectors and a partridge in a pear tree. At which point I politely ask, "Is there a specific type of cable that you're looking for? I can let you know if I have it or not."

RRR shakes her head and promptly walks away, leaving me to wonder what the hell has just taken place, and more importantly, why she didn't try and charge me for tidying up my stuff. Thank you mystery woman, wherever you may be.

Chapter 31 – Double Your Pleasure, Double Your Fun

Boot sales typically take place between April and October, giving us British folk a one in ten chance of not getting rained on. The nicest ones are from the end of June through to the beginning of August. Not only is there a better chance of good weather, but the sun is up when you arrive, and I can tell you from personal experience that setting up in the dark is a major pain. Granted, you also get lovely weather in August, but you also have a lot of people going away for their summer holidays.

The smart move is to commit to doing more than one boot sale in any given season, and it also makes sense to attend different locations too, as a lot of buyers tend to go to the same sale, week after week.

But in addition to increasing your sales chances, there's also something very interesting that happens when you do more than one sale.

You find more junk. In fact, you'll find a lot more.

In my most recent round of boot sales, I had committed to working three of them. The third was on a Bank Holiday Monday and turned out to be a serious waste of a morning, so I upped the total to four.

What was interesting was that in the first week I filled my car to capacity, had a great morning at the sale and came home. When it came to loading up the car again for the following week, I found myself going through new areas of the house that I had previously overlooked. The kitchen cupboards had tons of unwanted stuff in them, the coats cupboard had a veritable cornucopia of unwanted coats, and the corner in the loft where tech goes to die was positively overflowing with unwanted cables – no longer of value to me, but perhaps...

In weekend three, the same thing happened again. Kitchen gadgetry stashed in the utility room was cleaned, tested and put on display. The children finally accepted that some more toys were ready to move on, and so it continued.

The point is that getting swept up in car boot fever allows you to become just that bit more ruthless with your junk. Now some people don't need any help in that regard, but many of us are hoarders, and a good round of boot sales can be just the kick up the arse we need to get our houses in order.

In many ways, I like to think of it as the first step in prepping a room before paying a decorator to come in and do a proper job of making that room look nice. My DIY skills extend to flat-pack furniture and putting up the occasional shelf. If I'm tasked with painting a room, I will take four days to do what a professional can do in a single afternoon, and he or she won't have had to make half a dozen trips back to the shop because they forgot something, or roped their mates into helping because, and I am comfortable enough in myself to say this, I totally suck at decorating.

Chapter 32 – It's Not for Me

People are a funny lot, aren't they? In the ragtag world that is commerce, these same people seem to fall very neatly into two groups.

The first group see the price of something as a piece of information. Information to be contemplated, and then acted upon by either a progression to purchase, or the decision to withdraw, based upon a mutually agreeable set of criteria.

The other bastards see that price as a declaration of war. "Oh sure, SOMEONE'S going to be happy to pay £2 for that new pair of Reeboks, but it's not going to be me. Now let's see what you're really made of – we fight to the death." It really can get very violent in my subconscious – I should probably speak with someone about that.

Now we all know that negotiation can be a tricky business. Unfortunately, the hardest part for you as a seller is to recognise the rationale behind the buyers' eyes. I'll try to break it down for you:

Step One – I don't want to pay that price.

Yeah, there really is no step two on this one. You see, rationale, logic and good judgement really all pay second fiddle to the fact that some people, no matter how fair your price is, simply don't want to pay it. They have given no consideration to your circumstances, your cheerful demeanour, or the fact that £2 is actually a bloody good deal for a full-length portrait of Elvis. Their brains loop back to step one.

And these people are wonderful, because as soon as you ask them to explain their thinking, they come up with some of the most bizarre nonsense you will have ever heard, and whilst I would love to compile some sort of Top 10, I'll just settle for sharing one of my favourites.

The item in question is a set of espresso cups and saucers. This was a brand-new item – an unwanted gift that had sat in its box in my loft providing a safe haven to spiders and dust.

The customer shall be given the code SWN, which stands for Sorry, What Now? And I'm fairly sure you'll quickly see why.

SWN – "Alright mate? How much for the cups?"

Ahhh, he called me 'mate'. That international sign of fraternity that has existed between all men since we first crawled out of our caves and clubbed a passing squirrel to death for a mid-morning snack. Funny thing is that I really don't like being called 'mate' by perfect strangers, and yet in the car boot arena, that same guard comes down, and I find myself referring to others in the exact same way.
Other terms of endearment may well include Pal, Chief or Buddy. Spot every instance in this book and you could win a mystery prize. *

Me – "It's five pounds for that, mate." (See – it's like a disease.)

SWN – "Is it all in there?" Well you'd have to give a standing ovation to the balls on the guy that would sell an empty box for five quid, but that's not what he meant of course. By asking if it was ALL in there, he wanted to establish that nothing was missing.

Me – "Sure is, chief. Let me show you." (Oh good God, I can't stop myself.) I proceed to take out the cups and saucers to show that even the packaging material is still in there. I decide it's time for a story.

Me – "It was a gift, but the truth is that quite a few people had a similar idea because they knew I'd just been given a Nespresso for my birthday, so this lot just never got used."

SWN – "Five pounds yeah?"

You heard it, right? That little flicker behind his eyes that tell me his brain has just activated Step One.

Me – "Yes. Five."

SWN – "How about three?"

Me – "Can't really do that, mate. I checked online, and this lot goes for twenty quid, so five is really a fantastic deal."

SWN – "It's not for me, pal, it's for her." At which point he indicates his, let's say, girlfriend, who is standing right next to him and enjoying this little tête-à-tête.

Me – "Well how does that work then?" Now this might sound hostile, but the girlfriend and some other observers were giggling at this stage, as SWN knew that his argument held about as much water as a shopping trolley or anything said by Donald Trump ever.

SWN – "Hey?"

Me – "Well let's say you take this lovely lady out for dinner, when the waiter comes over with the bill at the end, do you point out that some of the food was for her and therefore ask if you can pay less?"

OK, there's a strong chance that this person has only ever ordered his food from a woefully undertrained teenager behind a counter, but I'm not here to judge. OK yes, yes I really am here to judge, but the analogy doesn't work if this guy's idea of a high-class eatery is simply a place where they give you cutlery.

Of course, I could have been much nastier and pointed out that asking to pay less for an item that you're about to give as a gift, directly in front of the person that's about to receive said gift, is decidedly lacking in class.

SWN – "Fiver then, yeah?"

Me – "Indeed. Thanks mate," and by then, we really were like blood brothers.

*There is no mystery prize, but I just hate it when people put that little asterisk next to a statement and then leave their poor readers desperately searching all the way to the end of the book for an explanation. See? I look after you like that. Help yourself to a Fruit Pastille. **

OK, look, to be clear, you'll have to go and buy those for yourself, unless of course you already have some in the house. I'm not going to give you any of my Fruit Pastilles. *

***I don't actually have any Fruit Pastilles, so if you are popping out, please can you get me some? Thanks pal.

Chapter 33 – The Camcorder

Like every exchange that I've covered in this book – this actually happened. Nothing has been enhanced for dramatic purposes and no people were harmed in the creation of this scene. Although by the end, you'll kind of wish they had been.

Unlike the clever acronyms that have been used throughout this book to describe my would-be customers, the muppet in this story will simply be referred to as Shovel, as that's exactly what I felt his face needed by the time he'd walked away.

I was selling a camcorder – yes, they do still make them. It had a little bit of charge left in it to prove that it was working, but only a little – and that will be important later on:

Shovel – "This camera?" OK, yes, I am going to offer a full and accurate transcription here. Shovel was not of these shores. I could have a stab at where he was from, but ultimately it just doesn't matter.

Me – "Yes, it's a video camera – high definition – good machine."

Shovel – "How much you want?"

Me – "Well I have been asking for eighty pounds, but people don't seem all that interested so I will now take sixty."

Shovel – "It work?"

Me – "Not really in my interests to sell broken merchandise – I couldn't live with myself."

Shovel turns it on and remember when I said that the thing about the charge being low would be important, well that happens now. It turns on, blinks that the battery is low and turns off.

Shovel – "It no work."

Me – "No, no, it just needs charging. Look, if you're nervous at all I would be happy to give you my details and if it doesn't work, full refund – no quibble at all." I should also stress that a very nice man in a neighbouring van was actually offering a charging service from his generator. When I say offering, I mean he was selling it, and for the right customer, I would have been happy to go and charge it up.

For the right customer. In hindsight I would have preferred to give my bank details to that nice Nigerian prince who just emailed me than give my address to this bloke.

Shovel – "You take forty?"

Me – "No. I've only just come down from eighty to sixty for you – I think you can do better than that."

Shovel – "Come on, forty."

Me – "No, no – saying the same price again but putting the words 'Come on' at the beginning is not really going to make a difference is it?"

Such a reaction may well have appeared impatient to some of you, to which I should explain. First, at this stage of reading you should clearly know that I have very little, if any patience for these people. Second, please bear in mind that this prick has been on my stall with this camera in his hands for twenty-five minutes. TWENTY-FIVE FRICKIN' MINUTES! Wars have been fought and lost in minor countries on the other side of the world. Babies born, love declared in front of friends and family, justice served, adversaries vanquished, theories proven and religion questioned, but I have missed all of it, because I have had to entertain the mindless questions of this discount-wanting, camera-hogging, soap-dodging, poor excuse for a human being. I can literally set fire to trees with the hatred burning in my eyes, but I keep my cool.

Shovel – "OK fifty."

Me – "You know what, I'm going to let you have it for fifty because you asked so nicely." Sarcasm is wasted on this guy, so I may as well have my fun.

Shovel then reaches into his wallet and pulls out £45.

Me – "We said fifty."

Shovel – "Yes, I will pay forty-five now and go home and test it and if OK, I come back and give you other five."

La la la la la la la. Dum di dum di dum di dum. Wee wah woh wah wee. La La La.

Now what just happened there is you witnessed my consciousness travelling to another plane. It's a magical and peaceful place where there is no money, no possessions and there aren't even any other people. It's just me, floating along on a cloud without a care in the world.

You've probably got a place like it too, and I imagine it's lovely. On this particular day, mine was a light purple colour. The air smelled of coconut and the only sound was that of a gentle breeze as it brushed against my ears before the silence chased it away.

It was important to go to this place because unfortunately, a very small piece of my mind was still back on Earth, at that very same car boot sale, and had just witnessed the same scene that I painted for you. So, amidst all of my calm, part of me was thinking...

DIE DIE DIE!!! You horrible little insect! You are a symbol of everything that is wrong with the world! Seriously? I mean is your pathetic existence so starved for attention that it felt the need to suck me down to its level for the past half an hour?!?!? What did you do this morning? Set out on a mission to be the biggest prick on the planet?? Congratulations Dickwad, mission well and truly accomplished! Now just allow me to demonstrate some small measure of composure whilst I dispatch you in a manner nowhere near fitting what a scum-sucking amoeba like you truly deserves!

Me – "I'm sorry mate, but this camera is no longer for sale."

Shovel – "Ugh?"

Me – "You've been here for half an hour and right at the point of agreeing on a price, you decide to treat me as if I am some sort of arsehole. I've been polite (good lord you have no idea) but I'm done with you. Now give me back the camera and go and bother someone else. Better yet, go home so that no one else here has to suffer the hell that is having to deal with you."

I never did sell the camera that day. In the end it went on eBay for £65. However, the small round of applause that I received from my neighbouring stall owners and their customers made it all the more worthwhile.

Chapter 34 – The Magical Piano

Many of the tales in this book were provided as some sort of cautionary tale. Realistically, they were put together as the thin fabric by which a series of rants on the part of a bald, middle-aged man are woven together, but hey – if you actually did learn something – bonus!

However, putting such educational aspirations aside, there are some instances where we can all take just a few moments to embrace our inner git, and laugh at a stupid person.

When he was much younger, my son was given a toy grand piano. The thing had about twenty keys on it and could play "Greensleeves" on demo mode, and to a young boy, this thing was magical.

Now, having just achieved a Distinction in his Grade 1 "not toy but actual" piano (Daddy is very proud) the magic had somewhat evaporated, and the piano was simply taking up space and doubling up as a shelf for other assorted crap. In short, it was time for it to go.

And so there it stood, taking pride of place at the edge of my stall because I knew that it would draw interest. Surely such an elegant piece of children's entertainment would attract the very cream of the intellectual elite to cast upon it their wise eyes and enquiring minds? Surely?

Nope. We got a monkey. In a pink tracksuit. With a tan – which no sensible person, or for that matter, chimpanzee would think was real. And hooped earrings, and...wait for it...because by now you are painting what I imagine is a fairly accurate picture...ready?...pushing a baby in a buggy! Yes indeed ladies and gentlemen, in the game of life that is Chav Bingo, we have achieved the equivalent of a single line, so let's carry on – we are now playing for a full house.

We're going to call this one PCB, which stands for Pure Chav Bingo. Now I fully accept that there may well be some chav-like ladies out there that might take offence at such a blatant tarnishing of their good name, but in all fairness, I have considered the demographic to whom this book is likely to appeal, and they are – quite understandably – just not in it.

PCB – "That real?"

Me – Now slow down, don't get ahead of yourselves. You all know what I want to say. Something whimsical along the lines of "Well you're not imagining it." You all know that I'm happy walking that thin line between well-observed sarcasm and flat out taking the piss. I really have only had a few seconds to formulate my opinion of this person and it's still quite early.

Oh, and I almost forgot – you can now tick off all four corners on your bingo card. Sure, I know she's only said two words, but they are delivered with all of the poise and grace of dragging the claws of a dead pigeon down a blackboard, so I'll let you skip ahead.

So many ways to respond to this person. Granted, it's taken you close to a minute to read these thoughts, but this exchange is happening in real time, and all with someone who, in my experience, is likely to have the attention span of a goldfish – and the skin tone to match. Plus, it's not like I want to alienate this person. After all, she might actually buy it. It's generally suited for children aged five and above so intellectually, she's well on her way to becoming qualified. I opt for an answer which is engaging enough to keep her there, but for the majority of its subtext to go way over her head.

Me – "Well it is a toy, but it is real."

PCB – "But it works though yeah?"

Me – "Indeed it does, let me show you." I then proceed to play a few keys and press the demo button so that we can all enjoy "Greensleeves" together, allowing me to think about Henry VIII and her to contemplate buying an ice cream.

PCB – "Do you have to plug it in?" Now for those of you that might have skipped ahead, we are in a field, and whilst mains electricity is available via the pylons nearby, when it comes to wall outlets, we are in unbelievably short supply. And remember, I have just shown her a working demo.

Me – "No no, it's battery operated, and they're all in there."

PCB – "Is it new?" There's no box, it's not very clean and has a couple of scratches on it. Only a moron would think...oh right, hang on.

Me – "No it's a few years old now, but well looked after."

PCB – "Alright fanks" and away she goes, allowing me to look at her lower back tattoo in all its glory. THERE IT IS FOLKS – WE HAVE A BINGO! THE 'TRAMP STAMP' HAS SEALED THE DEAL!!! STEP UP AND CLAIM YOUR PRIZE!

Of course, she never did buy the piano. One can only assume that, as it was getting close to 8am on a Sunday morning, that she needed to get home to catch up on all the episodes of Teletubbies that she's recorded in the week. So whilst I cannot put a monetary value on that exchange, in terms of brightening up my morning, it really was priceless.

Chapter 35 – Don't Boot Angry

You may well think, in reading this book, that I have a very little tolerance for people. That's not true. People are great. The rich tapestry that make up the population of car boot buyers were inspiring enough for me to write this book, so whilst I know none of their names, or know if any of them will ever read this book, I am grateful to each and every one of them.

But there's always one exception, and to make things even more interesting, this chapter is not about a buyer, but a seller.

You see some people just shouldn't do car boot sales. In fact, it would generally be considered better for everyone if they refrained from leaving the house altogether.

These people simply don't 'get' how all of this works, so they come to boot sales not to sell, but to do battle. They are a vacuum of aggression and negativity that, if left unchecked, have the power to suck all of your good mood straight out your arse and send it hurtling to the depths of hell from whence these people first held dominion.

Over the course of one weekend, I had the pleasure (and I use the term to mean the exact opposite) of having a stall very near to one particular lady (and again, using that word in its broadest sense).

This woman had the incredible ability to make everyone she spoke to instantly dislike her. People would ask her the price of something, she would bark a number at them, they would attempt to negotiate and she would snatch the item back out of their hands and tell them to go away.

It gets worse. If someone returned to her stall after previously not buying anything, she would tell them to go away again, pointing out that she had no interest in selling to them.

At one point, I actually heard one gentleman refer to her as a "miserable old witch", and you just don't expect to hear that sort of language from a priest, but there you go.

I simply could not understand how this person expected to sell anything at all, which was a fair question as she actually sold very little, preferring instead to commit to a roaring trade in misery and bewilderment.

And to top it all off, in one of her quiet moments, she actually came over to me to start bitching about all the people that kept coming up to her stand. Clearly my protection spells were not worth the paper they were printed on – thanks a lot J.K. Rowling!

The point of all of this? Don't come to a boot sale to do battle or make a profit. Come for the chance to engage with new and interesting people. Come to see your junk become another man's treasure. Hell, come because the van just twenty feet away from you serves a mean jumbo hot dog and a cuppa.

Now just in case my rants would lead you think otherwise, I genuinely love doing car boot sales, and I hope that you'll be able to find some joy in it too. Whatever you do it for – just enjoy it and let people see that you're enjoying it and gather just a few car boot tales of your own.

GLOSSARY

As promised, here is a breakdown of my three-letter codes for each type of buyer, placed neatly in alphabetical order. There's a good chance that you've figured out what the codes mean already, in which case you can think of this section as a desperate filler on the part of the writer, except that I'm not being paid by the word, so there's very little point.

Either way – enjoy.

3M – Marvellous Mechanical Machine. This really isn't someone that you're going to encounter on a regular basis, or perhaps even at all, but it was a fun story so I hope you enjoyed it.

CNB – Clearly Not Buying. It will be all too painfully obvious early on that this person is not going to be reaching into their pocket for that all illusive 20p piece any time soon. The trouble is that they seem perfectly pleasant and will happily ask you lots of questions about stuff which you just know they're not going to buy. Unfortunately, all you can do is nod, smile, and answer each question as it comes at you, and just hope that they'll give up and walk away soon. And however soon that is, it will still have felt like an eternity.

FFS – Exactly what you think it stands for. Some people manage to reach the pinnacle of stupidity and then, suspending all disbelief, actually find ways to be regarded as more stupid. These people should not be allowed to operate heavy machinery, go on trains unaccompanied and – and I cannot stress this enough – breed.

ILN – I'm Leaving Now. Any buyer with an overinflated sense of self-importance. You really should be grateful that they have condescended to approach your stall and even given the slightest thought to buying something from you. Don't you know who they are???? No, you don't, nor do you care.

JAP – Just a Plank. Other choice words would include moron, clod, idiot, or indeed a grunt in their general direction for those who have elected to regard regular speech as just too much like hard work. There's no excuse for this level of stupidity to exist in modern society. However, there are laws against sending them all down a mine somewhere, so I guess we're stuck with them, so just boil the kettle, hand them a Pot Noodle and see if they can work out how to make it before the water gets cold.

LBT – Loud, Big Teeth. On the surface, these people exude an energy which is bound to make you feel good. They have a smile that could light up a football pitch at night and a voice loud enough to be heard over its 50,000 spectators. Like I say – pure sunshine. But when it's 5.30am and you'd rather be in bed, this person is just the opposite of everything good. It's not their fault, they genuinely mean well, but there's no way on Earth that you're going to be able to match their energy, or at the very least to ask them to dial it down a little. It's a shame really, because under normal circumstances you could happily see yourself going for a drink with this person. Except these are not normal circumstances, and it's strange how the human mind can think of twenty-seven different ways to use a Barbie doll as a weapon. Just breathe.

MFS – Middle-aged, Foreign and Slow. Yep, that pretty much sums it up. Now to be clear, the slowness is not a product of a language barrier – that would be unfair. No, I've factored the translation issues into the equation and have still drawn the conclusion that these people must have eaten a good number of crayons when they were children. Or possibly adults.

MTV – Male Trader Vampire. These people are here to buy things from you cheap and early. They will invariably want mobile phones or electronics and they will not wait for you to get out of the car before asking. They are usually dishevelled (what's the opposite of that – shevelled?) and it would not be the worst idea for you to remain upwind of them. Their breath will be unpleasant, although that's usually masked by cigarette smoke, and they will be very direct – verging on rude.
To be clear – I don't like them.

NFP – Not 50p. I'm hoping you would have figured that one out by the time you got here. No matter what price you declare something is, they will respond with "Not 50p?" In fact, you may well be lucky enough to have them visit your stand more than once, so if you have a good memory for faces, you can actually beat them to the punch. When they ask you the price of something, respond with "Not 50p," and watch their eyes jiggle as they try to process what's just happened.

OAL – Optimistic African Lady. Her manner will be as bright as her outfit. She will be engaging and friendly – some may even say jovial. And then things will turn dark. Very very quickly. The moment she realises that she is not going to get the deal she wants, she will make you feel rather uncomfortable, almost guilty. Stand your ground – it's all a show. Cultural differences will make you feel that you are on the receiving end of an aggressive attack, but you're actually not. These are people that believe in straight talking and straight dealing, and you'll be showing respect if you act appropriately. Don't be rude, but don't be a pussy either.

PCB – Pure Chav Bingo. I'm pleased to say that I live in area where there exists a certain demographic. Young girls with voices that could grate steel, dressed in pink velour tracksuits, fake tans, massive, hooped earrings, hair tied back so tight that you can see their retinas, a tattoo at the base of the spine and of course, the obligatory pram. The men in their life are called Darren and are still in school – as indeed are they, but the school system has given up on them so much more than they have given up on it.

These people are destined for an appearance on a Jeremy Kyle show. For those outside of the UK, think of those shows where people that you would cross the street to avoid air their dirty linen in public. Every country has one, and ours are no better.

Now many people will tick some, but not all of the aforementioned boxes. To be a real PCB, you have to check all of them. Play along at home if you like – it's fun for all the family, especially Grandma, who in their case is usually about 34.

PFE – Pleasant, Fifties, English. As you venture out into the world of the car boot sale, you're going to find yourself dealing with the rich tapestry that is the human race. It would be very easy to form stereotypical opinions of people based upon such simple criteria as age or race, but to do so is just plain wrong.

A PFE will be charming and friendly – a genuine pleasure with whom to do business. Yes they may well attempt to negotiate, but there will be a shared understanding between you both that it is the nature of the sport in which you must both engage. Their name is likely to be Brian, Gerald or Malcolm, and their kitchen cupboards are never short of Chocolate Digestives for guests.

PGA – Please Go Away. This person is clearly very drunk, and as a result, has become very friendly. They will engage you in a conversation comprising very few actual words on their part, and whilst you must retain your composure for fear of getting punched in the face, you'll be privately praying to whichever deity takes your fancy that this person would please go away and rejoin the rest of their teeth.

PPM – Post-Purchase Millionaire. Any buyer who argues you down to the tune of 50p and then immediately starts browsing through all of your high-ticket items. A word of warning here, this happens A LOT. These people simply cannot help themselves. They may even have confessed to you that the reason they need you to lower your prices is because they simply don't have enough money left on them, which begs the question, how are they planning on paying for all the other stuff they're now rifling through?

RAM – Rather Aggressive Mother. It's easy to spot that these people are mothers because they have their children with them, although the way they behave in front of them could suggest that they had completely forgotten that. These people are looking for a fight. Not in the physical sense, but to them the negotiation is not a game, it's a battle, and their weapon and armour is comprised entirely of attitude.

It's a shame really, because these people have forgotten that all behaviour is learned. They are setting the most dreadful example in front of the children, and when those children turn into aggressive, belligerent monsters who think nothing of shouting at their own mother, that same mother will throw her hands to the sky and wonder where it all comes from. If you have any mirrors for sale on your stand, it might be a good idea to put one their way.

RRR – Rummage Rummage Rummage. Sadly there is little that I can tell you about this person. They will give nothing away. They will pick up every single item, inspect it, and then put it back in a different place, thus leaving your stand looking like a hurricane just went through it. They are introverted – finding it almost impossible to make eye contact, and may well acknowledge your existence with a small nod. Your enthusiastic greeting will be wasted on them, but that doesn't mean you shouldn't extend it.

SWN – Sorry, What Now? Not so much a type of person, but a reaction that you will experience at least once whilst on your car booting travels. At some point you will be presented with a reason to lower your price which makes absolutely no sense whatsoever. Don't try to wrap your head around it – it'll only make it worse. Just accept that there are some people out there for whom the sky is green and all the elephants smell like lemonade.

VIT – Vampire in Training. These people have not yet fully crossed over to the dark side. They dabble in the buying and selling of junk, but it really more of a hobby than a vocation. They are overly friendly and invariably loud with it. They will engage in friendly banter but they will have an agenda, so beware.

WFM – Words Fail Me. Obviously in most cases they don't, otherwise this would have been a very short, or perhaps non-existent book. Naturally many of the other codes can be applied to these people, who add to their overall ineptitude – a pinch of halfwit, a dash of numbskull and a soupcon of utter twat. Their questions will leave you dumfounded, but once you've established that these people have come armed with the IQ of cheese, it really is your right, perhaps even your duty, to have fun at their expense. Go on – you'll kick yourself later if you don't.

WSV – World's Smallest Violin. These people have a tale to tell. And tell it they will – all for the purposes of bringing your price down. It will be a tale of woe, and if you're not careful, you will fall for it. Now nobody is expecting you to be heartless, but just don't crumble and try to rescue the damsel in distress, because that is how they get you.

YTW – Young Tracksuit Wearer. I don't know why, but an awful lot of Eastern European gentlemen in their early twenties all wear the same style of tracksuit. Having spent little time in that part of the world, I can't really provide an explanation as to why this is, but at any given car boot sale, particularly in North West London, you do see an awful lot of tracksuits. The conversation usually goes the same way too – three words exchanged with you in English before they deliver an entire Ted Talk's worth to their friends (also in tracksuits) in their native tongue.

The good news is that these people invariably do buy, and don't even attempt to negotiate that much. I guess they're buying these tracksuits in bulk in order to bring the price down and thereby enjoy a higher level of car boot disposable income. Good for them.

Here endeth the lesson.

About the Author

Paul J Rose is a voice over artist who lives in Hertfordshire with his wife and two wonderful children. The wife is also wonderful.

For his next book, Paul plans to infiltrate the multi-million pound slimming industry by first consuming 300 donuts and then formulating some sort of plan.